Happy
Birthday, Dad!
Love,
Sarah
Ann, 1995

PICK OF THE LITTER

BOOKS BY BILL TARRANT

Best Way to Train Your Gun Dog

Hey Pup, Fetch It Up!

Bill Tarrant's Gun Dog Book:
A Treasury of Happy Tails

Tarrant Trains Gun Dogs

Training the Hunting Retriever:
The New Approach

Problem Gun Dogs

How to Hunt Birds with Gun Dogs

Pick of the Litter

PICK OF THE LITTER

BILL TARRANT

Illustrated by Eldridge Hardie

Lyons & Burford, Publishers

All inquiries should be addressed to:

Lyons & Burford, Publishers

31 West 21 Street

New York, NY 10010

Printed in the United States of America

Design by Lynne Amft Design

10 9 8 7 6 5 4 3 2 1

Articles in this book first appeared in *Field & Stream* magazine, copyright 1974 through 1987, by CBS Publications, the Consumer Publishing Division of CBS Publications; and *Field & Stream*, copyright © 1988–1994 by Times Mirror Magazines, Inc.

Library of Congress Cataloging-in-Publication Data

Tarrant, Bill.
    Pick of the litter / Bill Tarrant.
        p.   cm.
    ISBN 1-55821-345-7
    1. Bird dogs—Training—Anecdotes.   2. Fowling—Anecdotes.
    3. Hunting—Anecdotes.   I. Title.
SF428.5.T3813   1995
799.2'34—dc20   94-34323
                                                            CIP

This book is dedicated to four men
who are the

Pɪᴄᴋ ᴏꜰ ᴛʜᴇ Lɪᴛᴛᴇʀ

Duncan Barnes, Wilson Dunn,
Nick Lyons, and Bob Wehle

Contents

PROLOGUE

There's a mist in the hollow behind the place tonight and, up above, the moon has that glow of muted light seen through soft whiskers. Like a snowman who needs a shave. It's a wet moon announcing a wet tomorrow. I'll trudge to the woodpile in the morning to come back laden and huffing—and see my footprints in mud or snow.

There's a comfort to backtracking, you know? For one thing, it means you ain't lost. For another, it means you're going back to maybe someplace better than what you left to find.

Sometimes when you backtrack, you see and feel and smell things and times and places that were good, and the mind faintly forms them—you know it can't hold them—as they slip away like the mist that rolls past my window.

But that one moment of holding is golden and warm and beyond that bully capability of muscle or wealth.

Which sets me thinking. Why don't you and I backtrack twenty years of *Field & Stream*? Say we revive and relive some twenty tales of dogs and men and the things they chase (if nothing but pictures in their heads), the follies they fall into, and the empty bag they usually bring home. Or that rare day—that one in two million—where the light is right, the tree limbs are missing, the gun is swift, the dog calls the flush, and you'll never forget the soft wonder of that feathered lump in your palm.

Let's do it! For as I recall, and we'll check this as we go, there was laughter, gentleness, simplicity, God. There was downright stupidity and heroism and sharing and denial and defeat and love. Oh yes, love. That pooch-bellied pup with last-night's-ice-cream-carton smell. The four-year-old John Wayne of the bird patch with full-bored nose, banjo-strung pelvic-drive muscles, a great quiver of ruff above his neck when he slams to point. Or the tottering old warrior with locked hips, gimp legs, opaque eyes, matted hair, and watery eyes that says, "I tried boss and missed, but you know . . . I love you."

And men. The ones you go to field with. There ain't many. For that's the rarest of all loves. The way they flinch when you throw the safety, that red in the back of their neck when they miss. The thoughtful surprise of finding he brought a slab of ribs to heat on the truck's manifold. Or maybe just a PayDay candy bar he's carried all day. Or that other thing that happens—he put blanks in your gun when you laid it down to go see Miss Jones. That relentlessly dull hour when nothing flies and the sun comes high and piercing and you know the ducks will never leave the reservoir, but he . . . he begins, begins softly, a poem. And you thought he only read the classifieds for used guns. And here comes this poem of man and place and field and bird, and a heat comes through you the way raw whiskey sears your innards. You hush, "I'll be damned." But only to yourself—for you want to hear the end of that poem.

It's all there, you know. Down the backtrack. The finest dogs and the best men God ever put to earth. They made us giggle or gasp once, let's have them do it again. Come on, time's a runnin'. Oh, forget your damned compass. I know the way. Let's go!

1

Jimmy Kimmery and the Saddle Horse

The South is a never-ending novel.

You hear it in the hallelujah lament of a 200-pound black woman as she sings in a faded, clapboard church at the Y in a dirt road. Feel it in a prickly cotton patch when the temperature and humidity hit 90 degrees. Taste it in a praline. Share it with hard-hats in a roadside diner gorging on cat's-head biscuits and red-eye gravy.

It's there in a pirogue as you cast onto a turbid brown river flowing north. In the bawl of a hound back in the night timber, and in the lush grass on a hill at Shiloh battlefield where you never look down a brass canyon—there may be a copperhead snoozing in there.

It's in the wisteria and kudzu and gumwood trees. In the dark, overturned earth where a stone is never found. It's cursed to hell those nights you sleep naked under wet towels. Exalted in that frenzied craze of Saturday afternoon college football games. Go Alabama!

You recall it in a shot-down Doctor Martin Luther King. A risen Jerry Falwell. An indignant Senator Jesse Helms. A Randy Travis singing some dust-country ditty about lost love. You see it in an old man dipping snuff and spitting in a coffee can. A debutante in a white dress walking under crossed sabers. A stone-jawed, eight-year-old cadet marching at a military school. The clank of a New Orleans trolley. A yacht in your front yard from a hurricane in the Carolinas. A bobwhite exploding from a lespedeza patch.

I can gather more stories in the South in one week than I can in a year any place else. All you have to do is tap into the never-ending novel.

Join Wilson Dunn, of Grand Junction, Tennessee, a man whose hobby is guiding me to Southern storytellers (but then Wilson's joy is helping everybody), as he leads me into the Cotton Patch café at the intersection of Mississippi state highways 7 and 72, where we meet three game wardens who wait to take us coon hunting. This is the first time I'm introduced to Bully Palmer, hunter extraordinaire—storyteller supreme.

Like the drummer boy, I have only my craft to share: in my case, the art of the storyteller. Now, it is one thing to write a good story, but it is something entirely different and just as important to find and recognize a remarkable story in others. That's what I've done time and again listening to Harold "Bully" Palmer, the Marshall County, Mississippi, game warden who has led me day and night through slash, hollow, and thicket in search of coon, bobwhite, and turkey. Always going before me with a tale on his lips, an impish smile, and a broad-shouldered surge that separates the bush, Palmer also radiates a gentleness and charm.

It takes the Northen ear a few minutes to adjust to Bully's speech: it has that economy of the South where nouns are never plural, articles are often deleted, and there's a lot of "I saids," and "He saids," which accentuate the pattern of the speech's weaving. The voice itself comes in great expirations, great booms. Some words are slammed through the teeth so hard they explode; some come out—those with more than one syllable—like the word was a sentence.

"Bill," Bully says, "we was coon huntin' in the Mississippi delta at Vicksburg, and every time we would go, Jimmy Kimmery, another game warden I hunt with, would always want to ride a good horse. And I was carryin' him a different horse every time we go. So we got ready to go to Vicksburg one weekend and he told me, 'Look, I'm gonna borrow me a saddle horse.'

"I said, 'Fine, go ahead.'

"Well, he goes over to my partner and borrows a saddle horse. The horse never been broke. So we go to the delta: Jimmy Kimmery, Roger Elliot, a county official, and myself. No sooner we start out that night than the dog tree a coon. Now Jimmy's fussin' with that saddle horse, so we ride off and leave him. When Jimmy catch up with us, he give us a cussin'. He says, 'You all know this horse not broke and you all just run off and left me.'

"We say, 'Well, Jimmy, we won't do that no more.' We say, 'We'll wait on you from now on.'

"Well, I shot the coon down. The coon hit the ground, Jimmy goes up and catches the coon, walks over to his horse, and the horse kicks him on the leg. Right there Jimmy falled flat. He moan, '*Ohhhhhh*, he broke my leg. He broke my leg.' I say, 'Jimmy, did that horse break your—' 'Yes, he broke my damn leg.'

"I said, 'Well, let's go, we're gonna haf to carry you to the doctor.'

"But Jimmy won't go. Finally he gets up and he hobbles 'round, and he's thinkin' 'bout that saddle horse that kicked him and he walk up to that horse and just hit him in the side of the head—and the horse like to stomp Jimmy to death. I mean that horse is bitin' and kickin' and twirlin' and snortin' and by that time our dog had treed another coon.

"I said, 'Jimmy, let me help you on the horse with your leg broke and we'll get you to some help.'

"'Oh,' he said, 'I don't believe my leg broke 'cause I can put weight on it.' Well, I put him on the horse and he rides around there and we get to the tree where the dog had done treed. We gets off the horses and Jimmy walks up to the tree and looks up at the tree and I say, 'Jimmy, pull that vine.'

"So he grab the grapevine and pull it and a limb falls off the tree and hits him on top of the head. And when it do—you got to know Jimmy, he had a hair transplant. And them holes are all drilled in his head. Okay. Well that falling limb peeled that head skin from a few inches above Jimmy's eyes and it fell back . . . it fell back over almost down to his neck. And I told Jimmy, I said, 'Jimmy, let me roll that flap back over and we can pat that hair down without doing anything else to it.'

"Well, Jimmy he started walking around that tree where the limb fell off of like this here—all straddle-legged out and with his arms wavin' kind of stiff like a movie monster—when he suddenly hits the ground: *Whomp*! He just fell backwards and hit the ground and he says, 'It broke my neck, it broke my neck.' I said, 'Jimmy, did it break your neck?' 'Yeah, it broke my neck.' I said, 'Jimmy, no, it didn't—'

"'Yeah,' he wailed, 'it broke my damn neck.' He was laying there flat on his back on the ground. So we sat around there until about ten o'clock, and I got Jimmy's hair plastered back down and everything.

4

And I get him and put him back up on the saddle horse. By that time the dog had treed again.

"Well there was an old roadway there and a tree down there six foot across the stump, and it were hollow and we rode up there and I just stepped off and looked up in there and said, 'Yep, there a coon up in that hole all right.'

"Roger Elliot, what is the county administrator, he say, 'Get it.'

"I say, 'Let's tie the dogs first.'

"'No, don't tie,' Roger say. "I can stop up the hole. I'm going to stick the rifle up in there and shoot the coon, and I'll stop up the hole where the dog can't get in to him.'

"Well, he stick that rifle up in there and *Powwwwww*, and he missed the coon. The coon falls down, and there was some bark hanging down inside the tree. And the coon went behind the bark, and we thought the tree had a hole through it . . . for the coon disappeared. We all jump back and run around on the back side of the tree, and while we're back there my ol' hound run up into that hole out front and grab that ol' coon from behind that bark and away they start.

"I don't want my dog chewed up. I say, 'Jimmy, get the coon away from the dog. Get the coon.' Jimmy is runnin' on his broken leg with his broken neck and flappin' scalp and he reaches out for that coon and the coon grab Jimmy by the hand. And there goes Jimmy and the dog down on the ground. The dog had the coon, the coon had Jimmy, and Jimmy was goin' down the hill, and I was runnin' to grab the dog to keep the dog from pullin' the holes out of Jimmy's fingers. The holes where the coon's teeth were clinched. I mean, the coon's teeth were in the holes and it were chewing Jimmy's fingers good. The blood was goin' everywhere by that time.

"Well, Roger Elliot got down there and caught the coon around the neck with his hands, and he was chokin' the coon and Jimmy was gonna pry the coon off his left hand with his right hand. He headed his right hand down like that—*and the coon swapped hands*! Now the coon chewin' on the right hand and Jimmy is cussin' sure'nuf and I'm goin' down laughin'. And Jimmy look at me and he say, 'That ain't a damn bit funny to hear you laughin'.' But I couldn't help it. I was dyin' laughin'.

"Well, anyway we got that coon off Jimmy's fingers and we went out there and got us some tape and we taped all his fingers up. And Jimmy's horse now wasn't broke. So we loaded Jimmy up on the horse and we started out and there was some cut-over timbers—logs everywhere you look there—and we was going down through that. We all stepped across this one log, but the horse Jimmy was on reared up like he was gonna jump the log. He turned in midair, and Jimmy went down between two logs, his feet sticking straight in the air. And the horse— I was worried about the horse gettin' away from us for I knew Jimmy had to ride, what with his broken leg and all. So I got after the horse. And you ought to have seen Jimmy layin' down there between those two logs. He couldn't' get up with his head stickin' out and both feet stickin' straight up in the air and his hands like this. His hands lookin' in the dark of the night like a minstrel showman's hands with all that white tape on the fingers.

"By that time it was about eleven o'clock and I told them both, I said, 'Boys, it's time for this to be over with.'

"So, we loaded up and we finally got back to the house and the next day we worked on Jimmy all day, splintin' his fingers. And right now, if you see him, you can look at his knuckles and tell that he can't bend them. That coon eat his hands up.

"So, that's the story of that coon hunt, Bill, except for notin' the moral. And that moral is this: If someone ever offers to carry you coon huntin' with 'em and offers you a horse to ride, don't go tellin' 'em you want a saddle horse. Just look at Jimmy Kimmery. A saddle horse come near gettin' Jimmy Kimmery killed."

2

The Way It Was

Once again our setting is the South. Tell me, after you read this, where else could this story have been lived? Where else could it have been written?

Times have been hard for Thomas and Hazel Newton. But today it's raining and the skies are heavy gray. That prompts a kind of nostalgia, so they talk in soft wonder of what they've done and what they've seen.

I'm in a hickory rocker on the front porch, and side by side, as they have for fifty-four years, the two of them kick their toes to make the porch swing glide. I've come to Saulsbury, Tennessee, to talk to them about Sport, a legendary gun dog Thomas once owned, but the other memories come first this day.

Thomas says, "I was born May 30, 1916, right across the creek over there. About five and a half years later, when Hazel's folks took over the place from us, she was born in that same house. [By then, Thomas' family had moved nearby. In a lifetime how far have they moved? Three hundred yards?] I've known Hazel all my life. I had a hard way to go. Couldn't hear when I was a kid, and my daddy used to kick me and try to kill me because I couldn't hear.

"Daddy would hire me and my older sister out to shuck cotton for people and he'd take the money to buy whiskey. The year I turned eighteen, I took a horse and pulled stave bolts out of the woods all summer: I made $3.50 a day, and that was big money then. I never saw a cent of it. The ol' man, he'd go get it and maybe buy a few groceries and spend the rest of it for whiskey and foxing around. I got one pair of white pants with a black stripe out of that deal. That's what I got for working all summer."

He grows silent.

Hazel says in a firm voice, "Up until seven years ago we didn't have no water. [They'd been married forty-seven years.] We had a well, a little old dug well, which didn't afford enough water in the summer to even wash. If it rained a lot, we did. But anyway, I had to draw water for twelve hogs and that little pond out there went dry. It was a dry summer—the woods just burnt up everywhere. After Thomas had his heart attack he gave up and decided to have a well put down. That's why I had sewed quilts all my life; I was saving money because I was determined I was going to have a well some day."

Thomas readjusts his weight on the porch swing, takes a deep breath, and offers, "Never made no money farming. My big money came from trapping. I usually set my traps out around Thanksgiving, and during the war it was pretty good. I know I caught some fifty-odd foxes in the area of about $10 a piece. Then they went to $35. That was big money. But I got blood clots, and I didn't have no strength in my hands, so Hazel would have to go with me and tend the traps.

"I did all my trapping within a two-mile radius of here. Once caught forty-one coons in tunnels they'd made in the grass. Had to; they were eating up the corn. That was the year I made a little over $3,000 trapping.

"I used to skin beaver and stretch 'em round in an oval; most of them stretch almost round if you watch what you're doing. Hazel, she'd get a knife and work on them, taking that meat off the hide.

"But when you catch a mink the scent of it is worth its weight in gold. That's because they'll attract another male if he comes along. And female, too. But I never caught many females. Maybe 125 was the most I ever caught in my life."

Thomas and Hazel continue swinging. The chains squeak in the steel hooks that hold them. I clear my throat and say apologetically, "Thomas, the reason I'm here is to talk about Sport." Wilson Dunn, the driving force to build the National Bird Dog Museum at Grand Junction, Tennessee, and winner of the 1990 National Bird Dog Championship with Dunn's Fearless Bud, told me about this uncanny "natural" white setter with black ticking.

Thomas doesn't skip a beat. He gives the swing a kick and goes high backwards as he tells me, "I thought he was the best in the world at the time; he'd do everything. I got him when he was twelve days old. A bitch had ten pups and didn't have but eight good teats, so the people gave me one of the pups.

"I brought him home at two weeks. His eyes weren't open. Put him in a basket behind the stove. He hollered all night, and I'd have to come and give him some milk.

"And he started growing like wildfire, and I put him out. He got to killing chickens, so I hung one he'd killed on his collar. He never killed no chicken ever again. Matter of fact, to the day he died he wouldn't even eat a piece of fried chicken."

"Tell me about his hunting," I ask.

"Oh boy, I was fencing down here in the bottoms, and a covey was feeding down around there in the lespedeza. That afternoon, I left my wagon and team down there and went to the house to eat. I told Hazel to bring the puppy and my shotgun down there.

"She come down there, and I carried him to where that covey of birds was, and he froze solid. I could pick him up and turn him around, and he wouldn't move a muscle. "He's smelling them birds," I told Hazel.

"So I got my shotgun and moved on up. I kept walking around, and finally the birds flew up. I shot and killed one. We saw him go down, but when I went up there I couldn't find him. It wasn't nothing but one little patch of broom sage—hardly much bigger than this porch. But that pup just kept pointing like everything. And when we first stepped in there a rabbit jumped up and he never even looked at it.

"I told Hazel, 'I know the bird's in here.' I had seen a little feather and the pup was still pointing. I said, 'Go to the house and get some matches.' She come from the house, and we burnt that little patch of broom sage. When I saw a puff of blue smoke coming up, I walked out there and found that bird. Boy, did that puppy come running. And that bird was cooked, so I gave him to Sport.

"Yeah, ol' Sport. When he died, it was a lot worse to me than when I had to bury any of my folks. I went down there, and dug his grave, and cried like a baby. He always stayed with me, you know? He wouldn't follow anybody but me. If anybody wanted to go hunting with him, they had to go with me.

"If they killed a bird, Sport brought it to me. He wouldn't carry it to anybody else—no matter how much they tried to talk to him.

"He'd tree possums at night, and he was a good squirrel dog. He never would look at a rabbit. Everybody who ever hunted with him said there just wasn't anything like him hunting birds. He knew the days they'd be out. You know that? The days there was nothing there, he wouldn't hunt. A day like today now, with all the dampness and the good smells, oh boy, he'd be ready to go all day.

"I went down to my friend Bascom. He and his brother, Earnest, had been out hunting all that morning. They found two coveys and killed three birds. Now, I always carried my dog everywhere I went, so they asked me, 'Say, how about you being with us for a while with Sport?' And I said 'All right.' Sport found twenty-one coveys and worked all them singles in about three hours time. They killed a whole sackful of birds. I didn't have a gun, but Sport brought me all the birds.

"So when he died it was pityful. Now every time I go by that grave I'll say something to him. If he'd come up out of the ground now, I'd still love to hunt. Of course, I know that's impossible, but I still think about it. Bought a tombstone for him. He lived to be fifteen."

Thomas grows silent. He looks off at the rain and thinks. Finally Thomas says, "The old dog died in the summer. The spring before I was down on a little old pond where I keep my Canada geese; a covey of birds flew up, and I saw where they lit. I come to the house and got him. He had arthritis so bad he couldn't walk hardly. He went down there and found one of them singles. I shot it and killed it. He got that bird and brought it to me, then he started to the house and he pointed again. I walked up there, and I could see the bird before he got up—he was on open ground here. The bird flew up and I shot him and he fell in a great big ditch. Sport went right in that ditch after him. He couldn't get out, and I had to go down and bring both him and the bird out. And that was the last time he ever went hunting."

Thomas hesitates and says, "I had one good horse and one good dog in my life, and I guess that's about all you're supposed to have."

I look at faithful Hazel, who waited sixty-four years for running water. Who stripped the wallpaper off this little house and finished it with gypsum board. Who plants and harvests and picks and cans and tends the beet cellar and butchers. Who once ran the trap line, and who once could pick 360 pounds of cotton a day.

I look at Hazel and she smiles.

3

Let's Not Forget

Man Rand is an old black who may be the world's greatest bird dog man. But bird dogs are a Dixie institution, and sometimes rural black men still have a ways to go there.

   I knew Man Rand belonged in the Field Trial Hall of Fame. Never had a black man been elected. And I knew Man Rand would never make it.

   Now, a writer gets nothing done on a magazine without the power and consent of his editors and staff. Remember that with every story you read in this book. Always there were other people involved in that story getting to see the light of day.

   To the credit of Duncan Barnes, Editor of Field & Stream, he sent the following story back. I'd soft-pedaled my plea. Barnes said, "Strengthen the ending."

   So the story you are about to read ran in Field & Stream with that extra strength, and when the next vote came for the Hall, Man was overwhelmingly elected.

Southeast of Sedgefield Plantation's manor house is a memorial heralding an extraordinary gun dog Hall of Fame. The roll of honor is a celebration of the immortals Paladin, Rapid Transit, Ariel, Luminary, Timbuctoo, Superlette: dogs that won the National Championship, the Free-For-All, the National Derby.

These champions and others of equal stature were trained by Clyde Morton, who won eleven national titles with seven dogs.

At another cemetery a mile away lie Wrapup, Spats, and Allure, who together won two Nationals, one National Derby, and seven Free-For-Alls. These wins were posted by Billy Morton, no relation to Clyde.

The legend of this Alberta, Alabama, kennel runs through the initial owner A. G. C. Sage on to the present Jimmy Hinton of Tuscaloosa, Alabama. Together they had the two Mortons train for them, plus the initial helmsman J. L. Holloway.

Now all this is stunningly impressive and more than a little bit complicated to recount. Yet my emphasis here is not on the above-named men, nor the dogs. No. There is a silent, inconspicuous thread that runs through the fabric of these data and these laurels—a part of Sedgefield as sure as the winding lane to the manor house, the great, white-painted barn, and the continual call of bobwhite on the hills and in the hollows. And that continuity and that force is a slightly stooped, fluidly moving, soft-spoken, hands-in-pockets, seventy-two-year-old black man named Man Rand, Jr. He has put his touch of magic, his love, and his sagacity on all but two of the national champions cited above. He has not only hand-reared and partly trained all the other dogs on the Honor Roll, but scouted each of them to their championships as well.

In all of American gun dog history I can name no man who has figured into the making of so many champions as has Man Rand. He is, in my opinion, one of the most notable gun dog men America has ever produced.

It's early on a Saturday morning; the sun is slanting in a long angle through the trees. A mellow racket of pleadings comes from the leaping English pointers watching Man Rand go from one kennel gate to another with his pans of food. He speaks softly to each dog, they each form their bodies into the chain-link gates with love. Man pats them and chuckles softly. He shuffles on.

I catch him from the backside, unawares, and tell him I've come to write his story. He looks at me with dimmed eyes; they look that way of pond water with a skim of ice. His voice is honey-strung and cordial as he makes it clear, "Yes suh, that'll be fine. But it'll all have to wait until I care for these here dogs." I smile, patting him on the shoulder, and tell him that's the way it must be.

I wait in the barn on a sawhorse with a saddle blanket for padding. I watch the man move from gate to gate, from dog to dog. There is a small shed nearby where he goes to fill the pans. In that shed is a great oven left over from the days when Sedgefield baked corn pone for the pack.

When Man joins me he brings a red nylon check cord snapped to his star pupil, Alluring, who has just won the National Free-For-All championship and run in the Nationals. Her trainer, Billy Morton, probably Man's greatest fan (and along with Jimmy Hinton, one of his most devoted friends) enters the barn and finds a perch. Jimmy Hinton joins us to lean on the stairs to the loft. We all start talking in the hallway of the great barn.

It's suggested that Man show how he teaches pups to retrieve. Man leads the champion to the barn wall and ties her to an eye bolt. The man sits on a rickety three-legged milking stool, as he has for probably sixty years. He talks softly to the bitch, his hands stroking her. She lays her jaw on his thigh and looks up at him with claiming eyes. Man shows her the buck: a wood dowel with Xs of pegs at each end to loft the thing from the ground so a dog can get the thing in its mouth. Man throws the buck, and the bitch they say must one day win the National Championship makes a puppy move to pick it up.

You see, Man rode scout when Mr. Clyde won nine of his eleven National Championships. A scout, over-simply stated, keeps the vying dog on course. He does tons more, but all to that one purpose, to show the dog well to the judges. For Billy Morton, Man has scouted two more National champs. But before Clyde Morton died, he told Man, "I'll always be two Nationals ahead of you." Now the two are tied. Man wants one more win. To win! He must win, he says, he must win . . . and his voice trails off as he looks off to the distance and takes a shallow breath.

Man Rand, Jr., was born on Sedgefield Plantation in 1917. His father worked there: he was one of the men who shovel-by-shovel built the hill on which the manor house sets. When Man Jr. was about eight, he was told to sit at a gate with a switch and let the wagon horses in, but "whoop," as he says it, the bird dogs or field-trial horses from getting out. Man sat there for years as the plantation was built.

Holloway, the first dog trainer, took a liking to the slight lad (Man says he's 5 feet 7 inches and weighs 145 pounds), and he used to ride up to the clapboard and galvanized-roof plantation schoolhouse and hiss for the boy to slip out. As Holloway distracted the teacher in talk, Man slinked to the offside of the horse and climbed up under Holloway's hunting coat. Then the trainer would say, real loud, "Well, I got to be goin' on down yonder. . . ."

With the bird dogs down and running, young Man Rand would put his bare feet in Mr. Holloway's coat pockets and cling to the man's neck as they soared over the grounds. When a dog struck point, Holloway would leap to earth to work the dog at wing and shot while Man walked the horse forward so the man would not have to come back for him.

Later, Man was given puppies to walk, to introduce to man and land and bird. Later still, he was training from womb to tomb. The dogs won like no other kennel of dogs ever won. The owners and trainers would pose for the photographers with Man and dog, but when they handed their silver trophies and stepped into the limelight, Man and dog melted into the background to go sit on the horse-drawn wagon or later, inside the cab of the pickup truck. And as the record of wins grew, the owners and trainers and dogs were voted into the Field Trial Hall of Fame. (Billy Morton has still to make it, but should.) And the silent, out-of-sight black scout with the magic voice and hands that did to bird dogs what master sculptors do to clay would begin that next Monday morning with his feed pans and his cooing voice and his soft hands to groom, form, and love the dogs to more wins still.

I don't know for sure, but I think common reason would have anyone think that Man has stood and waited for some part of sixty years for a writer to show up and yank him from the fabric of his nonexistence and put the ink on him. To tell you of the endless days of whispering to dogs the ambitions he bore, the frustrations he endured, the never-ending hope that one day he too could receive and hang (that which he as much as any man who ever lived has earned) a Field Trial Hall of Fame certificate on his scanty cabin walls.

If gun dogdom won't vote him in, his dogs would. Dogs who knew the scout's voice and touch before they ever saw daylight, who sat with him in the barn with the buck, who walked the fields on ropes, who later cast to hell and gone with the frail black man riding a tornado of a horse so no dog could ever evade him.

Billy Morton sums it all up for me in one statement. He says, "Mr. Clyde didn't like Ariel because he wouldn't do anything in training. He would only perk up at a field trial with the horses around and the excitement. Yet, this is the only dog that ever won the National Championship three times, and Man Rand trained it."

There are Hall of Famers who did less.

Or as Hinton, the boss, says, "Man Rand just learned to think like a dog. He can ride up on top a hill and nine times out of ten look it over and say, 'If I was a dog, I'd go this way.' He's always right."

More than a hundred years have passed since the first field trial was run in America. Since that time the stalwarts of the game have elected professional trainers, their patrons, gun dog writers, noted gun dog breeders, landed gentry, seasoned amateurs, and other devotees to the Field Trial Hall of Fame. But never has a scout been mentioned, let alone nominated.

In this old world the hewers of wood and bearers of water also serve. Having served, they should be recognized. And should they excel, they should be honored.

Man Rand has earned the right to enter into America's Field Trial Hall of Fame. As an elector to that august body, not only does Man Rand get my vote, but I call upon my fellow electors to cast their ballots for this humble scout as well.

I know for Man this is a back-door hope, something not granted—not even considered—for his likes before. But the America of my pride has always awarded merit. May pride shine now.

4

O L ' G E O R G E

Terry Smith, of Savannah, Tennessee, was the finest young man I ever met. He affected my life deeply, and then, inexplicably, he was tragically killed in a car wreck at the age of twenty-eight. In this story, Terry and I go hunting with his next-door neighbor.

Me and Gipson Hardin meet out there in the dark at Joe Gray's café, just south of Savannah, Tennessee, on the old Pickwick highway. Meeting in the dark is called for when you hunt with a farmer. Farmers have yet to admit to the invention of electricity; they go to bed with the dying sun.

Joe Gray knows how to cook bacon and eggs and could go far if he'd put beds in there so a fellow could sleep till dawn. But not so. It's out the door to Gip's dung-colored Chevy truck that smells of gun oil and wet feathers. It's over the distant hills—racing the dawn with snoring dogs and faint green dashlights.

Then through a village with a Coke machine, two gas pumps, a big thermometer, a Royal Crown sign, and out over a rumbling wood bridge with a mule's skull hung from the superstructure. We're going up Morgan's peak, and Gip's telling me, "We don't hunt like foot hunters. We're road hunters. And we're gonna hunt that clear cut today. The dogs will run the fire lanes, and we'll follow in the truck."

Gip goes on, saying, "No other way to hunt this country. The timber companies just cut everything down . . . and it lays there. A man can't get over it. Why, they cut her to the stump, then go back with dozers and big V blades and cut the stumps. Looks just like you're gettin' ready for farmin'. Then they take a big ol' V8 and set a man on it, and he'll plant those little loblolly pine saplings as fast as he can pick- 'em up. They run two of those units, and they'll plant 10,000 acres a year.

"You can hunt these roads for about three years. The first two years in this knock-down timber ain't no good. But from the third year to the fifth year, you've got quail huntin' because the weed seeds have made plants and the pine are just little. I mean sure'nuf good quail huntin'. After that, the pine get too tall; it shade out the feed and you've got no more quail."

Dawn comes cold, windy, and gray. A dreariness lays on the land. And I realize—I'm with a road hunter. You know what we all say about road hunters! And there's three of us crammed in this pickup. Yeah, Terry Smith's in here, too. My young retriever training buddy who set this hunt up. I look out at the landscape: a raped and mutilated land. Bombs went off here. Gravel's been ripped loose, leaving gaping holes, and trees jut up at tortured angles. The dried weed stalks make the land look like a nail bed. I raise on one cheek to get off the seat belt hardware each man had thrown to center and take a deep sigh.

Gip stops the truck. He goes to the back to flip the latch on the wood crate that releases the dogs. He comes back with his shotgun: a Western Auto special. He's sawed the barrel off, and the front sight consists of a penny-pencil red eraser that is held in place on top of the barrel with electrical tape.

I try hard to ignore the land . . . and the gun. I ask about the dogs. I can't believe the dogs.

Gip tells me, "Oh, these dogs got real good breedin'. There's ol' Big Red. Friend of mine found him at the city dump, and I've been runnin' him ever since. Look at him. Don't you suspicion he's full blood?

"Then there's Gabe. Both he and George are full brothers. They're out of my ol' dog, Lucky. When Lucky got old I knew I'd need replacements; so a friend of mine found an ol' worn-out lemon-headed bitch, threw her in the barn with Lucky, and we whelped this litter.

"You'll have no trouble tellin' Gabe and George apart. Lucky, the old stud dog, he bit George's right ear nearly off when George was still a pup. And he's got more tickin' than Gabe. You'll see that right off. And since Lucky was half German shorthair and half English pointer, and since the ol' lemon-headed bitch was all English pointer— these brothers are one-quarter German and the rest English. Just real fine breedin'." Gip jabs me in the ribs and confides, "Their nose is the secret."

I sink farther in the seat. Two curs and a city-dump dog. I look at Terry in wonderment: *How could you have gotten me into this?* And Terry sits there, upright, his Model 12 between his legs. He says to me in chirp, "You all ready to shoot sumpun?"

The day grows grayer.

Then Gip starts the truck forward and rolls down the window, saying, "George! Git on out of there," and I see a great, angular dog clear the front of the truck. He glances back, and his face could only have been painted by Edmond Osthaus. Why, that dog's likeness hangs right now in the Ames Plantation, home of the National Bird Dog Championship. That dog posed for Osthaus seventy years ago.

I rise in the seat.

For this dog named George . . . he don't run. He moves, instead, with the precision and cadence of a hammer mill. And he must have pressure-sensitive feet—they don't seem to touch the ground. And there's no emotion to this dog. A craftsman going to his workbench without smile. Then wham! ol' George with his right ear gone slams to point—his tail angling off at eight o'clock.

"That's it," yells Gip and both pickup doors fly open. Gip and Terry run to point, Gip yellin' back, "These clear-cut quail won't hold. You better git movin'."

I'm falling out of the pickup, patting my coat for shells, mistakingly ramming two duck loads in the Browning over-and-under, running to point when *Brrrrr* . . . they flush. The birds come up like a tossed hand grenade; I fire and miss, then fire and drop a cock to the right. Three deer jump up behind the pickup and race across the road. George darts before me, fetches up my bird, makes two *glomps*, and Gip yells, "No, George, don't eat that bird." George spits out the bird at Gip's feet, and just like that he turns up the road and starts the hammer mill going again. No emotion, no wait for praise, no jockeying for a coffee break, no notice of the deer—just, "If you're gonna go with me, you getter get to movin'."

Gip tosses me the tenderized bird and asks, "You fire twice?"

I acknowledge I did.

"An' you got one bird?"

I acknowledge that to be the case.

Gip says no more till we get seated in the pickup. He stows the birds and says, "You been handlin' guns long?"

What is there for me to say? Court's been held at dawn on this dirt road and the verdict is in. Still, there must be some appeal: This is America! But before I can think of a protest, Terry yells, "He's on point again." Both pickup doors slap back, and the two men launch forward like Marines vacating a landing craft under fire.

Now, I've seen some bird dogs in my day. After all, that's my business; eyeballing dogs and puttin' ink on my findings. But folks I've never—and I mean I've never—seen a bird dog like ol' George, the one-eared road hunter of west Tennessee.

He's the king of the road, the chairman of the board. Like the Peter Paul candy bar wrapper Terry threw on the dash after lunch that says, "No artificial ingredients." That's ol' George.

Never have I seen a dog move so light on his feet. I truly think George could start huntin' Tennessee Saturday morning, do Arkansas that Sunday, and finish Oklahoma on Monday. Without lookin' to side. Without one word of encouragement. The fanciest thing I saw Gip do for ol' George the whole day was feed him a loaf of bread, fresh from the roadside grocery, right after lunch. Now I call that an easy keeper.

These Tennessee quail run, so Big Red and Gabe will let them flush wild to front. But that doesn't always happen with ol' George on point. He has a way of ramming that nose to 'em and keepin' on the pressure; he may run one continual contact—one sustained relocation—for a hundred yards. And he'll hold 'em so you can flush 'em.

And there's another thing about George I have to admire. He shows no prelude to contact. He's out there runnin' and not turnin' left nor right when wham, just like that, he hits the fringe of that scent cone and he's on point. There's no tentative sniffing, no testing the wind to be sure, no hesitation in launching to cover; matters not if it's a deadfall four feet high or barbed wire with briar—he's going over or through, and on point.

Now ol' George may not be a perfect bird dog. He may eat a bird.

He may only hunt roads and not be skilled at casting to objectives. And he may not be registered where you could get papers on his beget. But if you lay those objects to side, ol' George, to my way of thinkin', may just be the best bird dog in America today.

And it could be charged I saw ol' George on the finest day he ever had. We got up thirteen coveys from dawn till nine o'clock in the morning and eight more bevies the rest of the day. And each of the dogs were down about the same length of time and had about the same number of finds.

So, the truth of the matter is, if you're gonna be a dog in Gip's dilapidated box, you've got to be great to start with.

Yet, Gip tells a story that leads me to believe I may have seen ol' George on a typical hunt. Gip says, "I was huntin' with two guys who had four professionally trained English setters. I knew birds were in this field, but the four setters combed it and didn't get a point.

"So I let George go, and in just a few steps he had a covey locked. We shot seven birds on that rise. Then we did that two more times within a half hour . . . and one of the boys with the professionally trained dogs offered me his two setters and a pickup truck if I'd let him have George."

Gip didn't sell George that day, no. He waited and gave him away to a friend. Gip has a way of coming up with good bird dogs, no need keepin' one if a friend is out of dogs right at that time. Gip just borrows them back to go hunting.

On our way home that night I asked Gip how he trained his dogs. He told me, "I don't want an old dog to train the young'uns. So I let 'em all run where there ain't no birds. When I get that runnin' edge wore off, I may walk the pup, get him into birds. Lots of birds. But he's alone, where he don't pick up no bad traits. Then I start him in front of the pickup . . . he can't get away from me there. And that's the way I do it, an' once I git 'em started . . . why, they're easy to train."

That's right folks, it's the same way Babe Ruth hit baseballs. You just take a bat and stand at home plate, and when the pitcher throws the ball you hit it.

Now we're back in Savannah, and the dogs are coming out of their crate. And would you look at that! Ol' George is leaping for attention. Why that rascal, he wants lovin'. And I stand there in the dark and marvel at this enigmatic dog. Seldom seen another like him—no need for a kind hand till the chores are all done.

And that night, in Terry's house, in the big brass bed with the dust ruffle and the handsewn hatchet quilt, I go to sleep seein' ol' George out there on those high-ridge, clear-cut roads.

He runs without touching the earth, without looking to either side, a nose and four legs attached with a rope of muscle: his head down, his tail down, his body without bounce, his one good ear not even flapping, his lopped-off ear standing straight out, then *wham*! He stops in stride on point. Just like the transmission dropped out of a car.

Head still down, tail still down. No chrome. Not a '52 Cadillac, but a '42 Jeep. No flash. Not a tux, just bib overalls. No notoriety or advanced billing or laurels to post: just work all day for a loaf of bread at lunch.

But no more, George. That's all passed. The presses are going to roll on you, and several million Americans are gonna learn your name and what you do. For George, in those hills today, on those birds, in that cover, with that wind, you were the greatest bird dog I have ever seen. And Gip may think it's "Just real fine breedin'. The nose is the secret." But George, I saw secrets in you today you ain't yet pointed out to Gip.

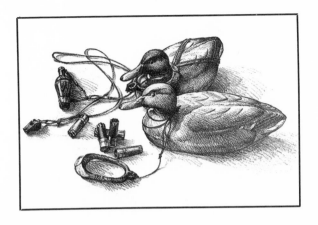

5

THE HUNTER WHO
TRAINS GUN DOGS

You *caught a glimpse of Terry Smith on Gip's road hunt, now let's meet him head-on. Terry was a massive man—he couldn't find a hat to fit his head nor a shirt to fit his neck—who never encountered a hardship while hunting. Ice, mud, rain, sleet, hail—no matter what, Terry was just glad to be alive and be afield.*

He loved God and family and friends, kept all the faiths, and made everybody feel like they were worth something.

He attended Memphis State University on a javelin scholarship that allowed him to earn a bachelor's degree in American history. His delight was being a tour guide at the Shiloh battlefield, but the work he took for pay was as a guard for the Tennessee Valley Authority.

Terry was my friend, and I will never recover from his death.

I know men who figure hardship to be a melting triple-decked ice cream cone: it's dripping all over their hand and they can't eat it fast enough.

But what is real hardship? Consider Chris LeDoux of Kaycee, Wyoming. (Twenty years after I met him he became a popular western singer when Garth Brooks put the spotlight on him.) Although he suffered from a broken collarbone, he rode ten bareback horses at the National Finals Rodeo to win his world championship belt buckle.

Or my Honolulu friend, Field Trial Hall of Famer and Weatherby hunter of the year, W. T. Yoshimoto. He was scheduled for Marco Polo sheep, but broke a leg. At the same time, he came down with black-water malaria. Did he cancel? Nope. What's hunting at 21,000 feet to a sixty-six-year-old cripple with malaria? Yoshi went and got the sheep.

Or junior college All American football guard and former high school athletic director Jim Culbertson of Wichita, Kansas. Jim once walked me so far in the gunk of Cheyenne Bottoms that I couldn't take another step. No mind. Jim just plopped me on top of the decoys in the little plastic boat he pulled and glomped on another mile. I was glum with my showing until Jim's retriever jumped in the boat with me. Even the dog had had enough.

But for just being totally immune to pain or fatigue, there's nobody like rookie retriever trainer Terry Smith of Savannah, Tennessee. He may come closer to being the bionic man than any I've ever met.

We were hunting a Stuttgart, Arkansas, pond; Terry was walking away from the blind when he was caught in the open by a ragged wedge of mallards that were rubber necking our decoys, looking for a home. Terry dropped rump first into the marsh—right up to his armpits in ice water—and began blowing a Reelfoot highball. I couldn't believe it. There are such amenities as creature comforts. And now he's going to hunt all day in wet clothes? With this cold wind blowing?

I charged him about it, saying, "You're sittin' in the water. That's incredulous. Nobody just sits down in the water in December."

Slowly he rose, like some lost link in man's evolution, the gray water pouring from him and overflowing his fireman's boots, the hanging strands of buckball brush and nut grass sliding away in an ooze. He said, "What's that got to do with it? We're duck hunting."

Now we're in a duck blind in west Tennessee, and the ducks must still be up in Illinois. The sky is bare of everything—even clouds—and Terry is bent over, sitting on an upturned bucket, carving a .58 caliber Civil War bullet he found at Corinth, Mississippi, into a cross for me.

Terry is over six feet tall and weighs some 250 pounds. Four years ago he was hurling the javelin and discus at Memphis State University. I've heard he threw them far. But I figure now he could toss 'em over the county line. Such a big man looks funny sitting on a little bucket. He holds up the bullet and asks, "How's that?"

"Fine," I tell him, but I'm thinking, *carving lead sure must be hard on knife blades. Yesterday he carved me a dog whistle out of a deer antler.*

As Terry carves he talks, and I scan the sky for ducks. He says, "This big, fat guy from the city asked me to train his dog. An' I guess he got to thinkin' about it, for come summer here he comes to see how his dog's doin'."

Terry stops his story and asks, "You all hungry?" I shake my head no, and he grudgingly goes back to whittling and talking.

He says, "So I take him and the dog down south of town to a slough. It runs through some cultivated land, but there's hardwood trees still around the slough, and the Tennessee River runs along the side. It's a good place to hunt ducks during season.

"An' doggone if I don't go and get that Jeep stuck. I mean stuck clear up to the bumper. Well, I wander off and rip out two fence posts and bring 'em back and pound 'em into the ground and hook my winch on 'em and out jumps the fence posts. So I know we're stuck.

"I tell this guy, 'We gotta go get a tractor.' But he don't want to stay down there in those bottoms alone. So I told. . . ."

"Why?" I interrupt.

"Why what?"

"Why didn't he want to stay there alone?"

"I don't know," exclaims Terry, waving the knife, "who knows why some city people do what they do."

"Go on," I tell him.

He continues, "So I told him we're gonna haf to swim this slough. I asked him if he could swim, and he said, 'Yes,' and I said, 'Let's go.'

"So I took my boots off and put 'em around my neck. I held a shotgun in my left hand and sidestroked with my right. I looked back there behind me—he was comin', just a dog paddlin' with his head up out of the water with a big, thick wallet chucked in his mouth. Looked like a Lab. A big, fat Lab comin' across there with a trainin' dummy in his mouth.

"We got to the other side over there, and I put my boots on and we commenced walkin' to the farmhouse to get the tractor. Now get this, this human Lab's doin' all this good, real good, but we had to stop about every 200 yards because this guy rubbed blisters. Just rubbed his ankles raw in them wet boots. You can imagine what it was like. He finally kicked his boots off up there and decided he'd walk barefooted on that gravel. He cut his feet all to pieces."

Terry concentrates on his whittling and says, "We got up there and got the tractor, then we come back down and pulled the Jeep out. This guy says to me, 'You're a maniac.'

"That's what he said. An' he told me he was takin' his dog home with him. He wouldn't leave it with no maniac. And he did. He took that dog home." Terry holds up the carved bullet. "How does that look?"

I'm laughing too hard, feeling too good, to comment on the bullet.

Terry's just the kind of guy most people would want to train their gun dog—if only they knew what a gun dog had to know. Primarily: terrain, cover, mud, sloughs, and heavy timber; cattle, highways, gravel, and train tracks; and—well, just all the things that composes a gun dog's workaday world.

Who could teach that better than a hunter?

Where could the dog go he wouldn't be followed? Some other trainer might correct an errant dog with a distant (and dry) electronic shock collar. Not Terry. He'd just swim after the dog, and when he got to him, he'd dog paddle and talk to him. As the dog zigzagged through flooded tree snags, Terry would tell the handler to take that whistle and stuff it with Skoal, then he would just knock a few trees down as he made his way in pursuit. Some people just don't know. *Maniac?* Hardly. *Outdoorsman,* Yes!

It may be that some people confuse being tough with being mean. Like they confuse being gentle with being weak. But I've met the world's great gun dog trainers. The national winners, the world beaters, the immortals. I've found some who are mean, and I've found too many who never even pet a dog. And there are others who just don't take to hunting.

Not Terry. He lives for the hunt. But mean? There's not a mean bone in his body. I've seen Terry with tears in his eyes because a dog got hurt. I've seen him overcome with sorrow because a dog failed a test. Not anger, sorrow! I've seen Terry fidget in an airport baggage line waiting for me because his dog is out in the Jeep in the parking lot and something might happen to him. I've seen him stop after a hunt and buy hamburgers for his string.

But if Terry is going to sit in ice water, the dog can, too. If he's going to swim the Tennessee River, they can swim it together.

It may be the client who wouldn't stay alone in the bottoms felt Terry was abusive and inconsiderate to man. Probably was. But not in

Terry's thoughts. He just had to go get a tractor, and going through a slough was the shortest route. Besides, what's that got to do with training a gun dog? The client could have sat in the Jeep.

A gun dog's world is raw nature. It's a world of snags and saw-briar and ice and cottonmouths. Worst of all, it's the debris of man: abandoned trotlines, forgotten varmint traps, barbed wire, broken bottles, and those damndable electric fences. The dog better be tough, and he better be trained tough to survive it all.

I'm seeing way too much circus-dog training (especially in the retrievers). I'm seeing dogs trained to make differences that don't make any difference. I'm seeing field-trial handlers who don't know a badger from a bagel. Cream cheese on a beagle?

I'm seeing dog trainers who do too many things remote controled—and electronic, gimicky, and manmade. Not taking the dog to nature to do natural things. Instead, they train the dog in concocted torture chambers to avoid traps set by field-trial judges.

What's any of this got to do with a day's hunting?

And maybe most important. I'm seeing too many gun dog trainers who never go hunting. Their lives and their gun dog training are like a game of chess: go to field or to war but never a shot is fired. Their interest is to checkmate the bird, huh? Not to shoot him and take him home for dinner?

Actually, there's only a handful of Americans vying for silver on the mantle instead of meat on the table. But the aesthete's field-trial game seems to set the standard, and it surely gets the notoriety. The meat dog is too often considered riffraff in the world of blue ribbons and blue bloods.

Well, I wonder. On a day's hunt, which of the two would get the job done? The one trained by a hunter under hunting conditions to hunt or the one trained by the mechanical trainer who engineers dogs to avoid a judge's hazards?

Personally, I go with the hunter. Always have and always will. A man who knows how No. 4s pattern and how to tell a gadwall from a baldpate in dawn's faint light, how to lay out a decoy spread and build a blind and blow a call and pluck a duck.

There are few Terry Smiths left on earth. And one reason for this is other boys just never had a chance: it's hard to become a bird hunter when all you know is sparrows and concrete, boom boxes and skate boards.

Terry tells me, "I started hunting when I was eight years old. Went with my dad and uncle. Then Mr. Price—he runs the service station in Savannah, I used to pump gas for him—he'd take me huntin'.

"When I was thirteen I started goin' alone. Had an ol' mare named Dee. I'd saddle her up and toss a tote sack of decoys on her back, grab my gun, and we'd go three miles south of town in the dark.

"Them decoys was somethin' else. I had four or five outcasts that people had thrown away. You know, like maybe they had the bill busted off.

"I didn't have no hip boots or nothin'. I'd just slosh out there in my tennis shoes. Put those decoys out. And I had a little ol' Lohman call. I'll never forget the first duck I shot alone. She was a big ol' Suzie. She looked like a 747 comin' in there on me. And I got her. I had an ol' single-barreled three-inch magnum Harrington & Richardson. An' I got her.

"There was no way I was gonna stay an' get another duck. I ran into that pond and got those decoys and that duck. Then I got my gun and jumped on ol' Dee and ran her all the way home. To show my mommy and daddy." Terry laughs, laughs and pulls Dixie, the young Lab bitch he's working, to his side and thumps her right chest with his flat palm.

Then the duck blind is silent and he says, softly, "I been ruined ever since. That ruined me. Sure did."

I smile and tell him, "Done in by a gal wearing a feathered bolo named Suzie." Terry nods his head in affirmation and adds, "Been married to her ever since. Hope I am the rest of my life."

And how prophetic he was when he added, "But there'll be some city types who want to divorce us."

I lean back in the blind, look at the young man carving the bullet and acknowledge those frayed cuffs, the mud-caked knees, that old Model 12 with the bluing all worn off. And he blows a call like he's got smelter bellows for lungs. Twenty highballs without taking a breath. And that ammo box he carries with him, filled with Beanie Weanies and sardines.

That's the menu of an itinerant farm worker—or a man you'd want to train your gun dog. If you wanted a gun dog for sure'nuf hunting.

6

B LIND F OOLS

Alice in Wonderland fell down a hole and entered another world. I would do the same thing every time I'd enter a duck blind with Terry Smith and his topsy-turvy friends.

All my life I've heard the expression *blind fools* but I didn't know what it meant until I crawled into this duck blind in west Tennessee. The Professor of Chromonology is in here, along with the Shotgun Contractor, and Colonel Goodwrench. There's also an old Lab in here, named Duke, but Duke's no fool.

Before the Professor got academic, he was known in these parts as Bruce Northcutt of Reagan (pronounced Ree-Gan by these Dixiecrats), Tennessee, a member of the pipefitter's union who deeply hoped no pipes would need fitting during duck season.

But Bruce hasn't seen many ducks these past two years—they've skirted this flyway, so it's been a lonely and fruitless vigil. He's pipe-dreamed his time away in this blind by establishing his imaginary School of Chromonology.

"With that degree," he tells me, "you meet the finer people." And so saying, this plumber with a poet's bent—a poet's and a rake's—winks his right eye and clucks his cheek like he's starting a horse.

"You see," says the Professor, "at a School of Chromonology young minds can be taught to chrome bumper hitches, eighteen-wheeler exhaust stacks, and running boards on horse trailers. It's all exotic stuff."

The Shotgun Contractor is Terry Smith, of Savannah, Tennessee. a rookie retriever trainer. The Contractor carries his gun wherever he goes, for he's always saying, "I'd sure like to shoot somethin'."

The other day the Professor and the Colonel (we'll meet the Colonel in a second) complained to the Contractor that the buckball bushes tied about the floating blind were too high. They couldn't see well through all the sticks, and when they stuck their guns through to shoot a passing duck the gun barrels hit the limbs.

Whereupon the Shotgun Contractor yelled, "Ge'back," as he blew a barrage into the buckball bushes, prompting the Professor to say, "You're a regular reload pruner, ain't cha?" And Duke, the Lab, crawled under a bunk in the back of the blind, making moans of forbearance, his paws crisscrossed on top his long black nose.

Earlier this week the Contractor and I were moseying about his steep-banked, timber-tangled farm (he says of the place, "It's good for nothin' but quail huntin'. A place like this just holds all the other places city folk says important together. I prefer the holdin' places.") when I noticed the hardwood saplings strangled by honeysuckle. The choke-vines spiraled the saplings, making of them long thin corkscrews.

"Oh, how I'd love to have those for walkin' sticks," I said. And the Contractor yelled, "Ge'back," as he blew them all from the ground with his Model 12.

Now the Contractor is saying, "I don't know why we ain't gettin' no ducks in here, but I'm thinkin' those decoys floatin' out into the honey hole ain't right. Where's there a place for the ducks to land?"

And Colonel Goodwrench (we'll finally meet him) replies, "Maybe so. Let's get in the boat and go rearrange the set." For that's how Colonel Goodwrench got the last half of his name: he's always fixing things. The first half of his name comes from his cooking things, for there's a Colonel over in Kentucky who cooks fried chicken.

But the Contractor places little value in the Colonel's suggestion and says, "No need for that, I'll just blow to the bottom those decoys that have drifted into the honey hole." He raises his shotgun, shouting, "Ge'back," but the trigger's never pulled.

The Colonel is off his bucket in a flash and has the Contractor's arm in grasp. For the Colonel gathered all those gallon plastic milk jugs and painted 'em black and tied 'em with anchor cords and weighted 'em and tossed 'em about the blind.

The Colonel, who is a tall, thin man with that sober disdain of a bank vault, tells all of us, "Don't shoot no more of our decoys. You know how much trouble they are to make? Why, it took me a year just to learn how to paint 'em. Latex won't work on 'em, you know that? They take flat-black enamel. That's what holds."

The Professor, who's philanthropy is to de-starch the Colonel so he can bend to the rapid-fire manner of the Contractor, says, "When I get my school started we'll chrome 'em. That'll hold, and the ducks can see 'em."

The Colonel sinks back on his bucket, defeated by the thought. For outside this duck blind, he's known as Mr. Carter to his high school biology students, Don Carter to the boys at the feed and seed where he buys supplies for his three farms up by Sardis, Tennessee. Yes, outside this blind, the Colonel has respect. Out there they wouldn't talk to him about chromed decoys.

By now, Duke—the Lab—has crawled from under the bunk in the back and sits beside me, begging for beef jerky I always carry in my hunting coat. I look to see the necktie again—the necktie around Duke's neck. It's dangling in the black water that stands 2 inches deep in the blind. "Why's Duke wearin' that tie?" I ask the Shotgun Contractor who owns the dog.

"Cause yesterday you told us about huntin' over there in England, and how all those gents wear neckties. So I just figgered we'd dress up, too. So's not to let no Englishmen git ahead of us." And so saying, the Contractor zips open his camo jacket to display a necktie in floral explosion hanging over and down the front of his bib overalls.

I tell him in shudder, "That's incredulous."

And he beams as he pokes the Professor in the shoulder, saying, "You hear that? It's in-cre-ju-less. That's what it is."

The Professor pooches a cheek like he's workin' a great chaw of tobacco and says in breezy tone, "That's as good a word as ha-bi-tat, ain't it?" The Professor turns and tells me, "That's the word you taught him yesterday . . . now it's in-cre-ju-less and ha-bi-tat." An' that's what we got here, right?" He sweeps his hand around the duck blind.

I look about the sinking blind—the muskrats have burrowed into the Styrofoam underneath and we are going down—and I see the scattered debris. It would be against international law to tow this thing to sea and abandon it.

But the Colonel, who teaches high school, thinks they're belittling me with their jests, so he leaps up saying, "Oh, don't act so dumb. This man can teach us somepun. He's been places where they really hunt."

"We know that," chides the Professor. "You always readin' those outdoor magazines. That's your problem, you know it? You want to learn too much." And turning to me he discloses, "Why the other day he was readin' about elephant huntin', and he's gettin' ready for it if it ever comes to west Tennessee."

"I'm not listenin' to you no more," says the Colonel. He drops back on a bunk framed of two-by-fours, pulling his billed cap down over his eyes, stuffing his hands deep in his jacket pockets.

The Professor laughs and says, "He's too serious. Serious as a heart attack. That's his problem. He asked me the other day what kind of duck it was that flew over, and I told him it was a calapegis. They're rare, you know? And he went home and looked in two dictionaries and couldn't find that duck. Then he looked for it down at the high school." The Professor slaps the tops of his thighs with flat palms and chuckles.

"But you spelled it!" charges the Colonel, raising waist-up from the bunk.

And the Professor tells him, "If I spelled D I D D I L Y would you spend a day lookin' for it?"

The Colonel stands now, sets his cap square on his head, tells me in firm voice, "He never lights you know? Always got his head in the clouds like a pintail. Why, that duck is born, breeds, and dies without touchin' ground. He's the same way."

The Contractor is listening to none of this; he says in grim voice, "I'd sure like to shoot somethin'." You see, the Contractor is in a time warp: born 150 years too late to be the mountain man he should have been. "Of the hunt, by the hunt, for the hunt," is how he would have said it if he'd been Lincoln. Of the table, by the table, for the table is how he views a duck. Terry loves to eat.

Colonel Goodwrench looks at the Contractor with sympathy and announces, "I shot a swamp rabbit the other day—"

He's interrupted by the Professor asking, "One of those orange rabbits with the Day-Glo ears? Long as a hoe handle?"

"Yes, the orange rabbits with the Day-Glo ears," parrots the

Colonel. "I shot him in the garden right behind my house. You know, that thing weighed nineteen pounds."

The Contractor maintains his vigil of the duckless skies as he intones, "Was he eatin' a three-pound carrot when you shot him?"

"Come, come now," submits the Professor of Chromonology in soothing voice, "No need for that kind of exaggeration. It's opposin' to my ethics. I don't go for that lyin'. No way. It's the code of the family. Why, you know," by now the voice is an undulating drone, "my granddaddy was really like George Washington. But it was a little different. George couldn't tell a lie; my granddaddy could, but he wouldn't. That was the main difference between 'em."

Colonel Goodwrench finds something to lean against, his body language saying, "This is going to take a long time." But the Contractor will have nothing to do with it. He says, "it's gonna git cold and then the ducks will come." And the Professor, still in organ tones— those deep tones you make with your feet at the Hammond—says, "Cold? Why it's not goin' to get cold. Not for me, anyway. Why, you know I've seen it so cold that a beagle had to use jumper cables to start a rabbit?"

The Colonel stands from the post he chose to lean against and shedding his reserve assures all of us, "Why, that's not cold. I'll tell you cold. Last year the thermometer dropped. I ran outside to get some wood, but it was all covered with ice. I got that wood into the fireplace and got it started. But come morning, you know what? The wood was completely burned up, but that ice was just laying in there on the fireplace floor."

The Shotgun Contractor says, "If I can't shoot nothin', I'm gonna take a pine board and paint a solid black circle on it and hang it over a wood duck's hole. That wood duck will fly in there and break his neck. And I'll put a net on a handle under the board, and I can hunt ducks while I'm home asleep in bed."

40

He turns to me and asks, "You think that'll win an award?" He's very impressed with the *Field & Stream* pins that the magazine used to give each year for the biggest bass, biggest deer rack, etc. I guess those pins are the only visual thing he could covet that might show the dedication of his life to the hunt.

"I have nothing to do with that program," I tell him. Then I ask, "Would anyone here care for tea?"

Only the Shotgun Contractor answers, saying, "Sure. If you'll fix it, I'll drink it."

It's fifteen minutes later; I'm sippin' Earl Gray's blend, sittin' in the back of the blind when I say to the Contractor—since he's so taken with the English and all—"After tea would you care for some croquet?"

The Contractor looks at me with a blank expression, then blurts out, "Sure, if you've got any with you."

And I hear the Professor of Chromonology fall into the black water—he's slipped from his bucket in laughter, and Colonel Goodwrench sticks his head into the back of the blind but can't think of anything to say.

The Shotgun Contractor asks, "Well, we gonna eat any of those fish croquets or not?"

And I turn from him to see Duke sitting there with his necktie hanging in the water, and I ask, "Duke, have you read any good books lately?"

7

Ben Lilly

F*unnin's great. I'll always love the blind fools. But there are also serious stories that must have the ink put on 'em.*

It came to pass I discovered that the greatest outdoorsman who ever lived was being maligned by the popular press and by a noted Southwest scholar. But the outdoorsman was dead. He couldn't speak back.

I decided we'd do it for him.

Welcome to the incredible world of the toughest rough-out of all time. And note this: Slaton White at Field & Stream *edits my copy for that magazine's ten million readers. So he often takes out an overhand right I throw at institutions or individuals who are harmful to hunting and fishing (in good journalism such comments are best reserved for the editorial page). But the stories in this book are unedited. All those haymakers are left in.*

In the Southwest corner of New Mexico, a half-hour drive north of Silver City on State Road 15, just at the entrance to the Gila National Forest, near the confluence of Bear and Cherry creeks, there's a portable toilet provided by the Feds for passing tourists on which some scrambled-brained ass (there's a left hook) has spray-painted, "Ben Lilly was a killer of wildlife."

Park your car and walk up a gritty path through claw brush and dusty pine to the west, and you'll break out on a vista to see Arizona standing smoky and lavender forty miles away. To your left will rise a jumbled lump of lichen-covered lava rock five times your height. On that rock there's a bronze plaque depicting a man under a limp hat; he's wearing a cleft beard that forks about the third button of his shirt. Flanking the man to the left is the head of a mountain lion, to the right a bear. Beneath the three of them is this inscription which happens to be true:

1856–BEN V. LILLY–1936

Erected 1947, by Friends

Born in Alabama and reared in Mississippi, Ben V. Lilly in early life was a farmer and trader in Louisiana. But he turned to hunting of panthers and bears with a passion that led him out of the swamps and canebrakes. He drifted across Texas, tramped the wildest mountains of Mexico, and finally became a legendary figure and dean of wilderness hunters in the Southwest. He was a philosopher, keen observer, naturalist, a cherisher of good hounds, a relier on his rifle, and a handcraftsman in horn and steel. He loved little children and vast solitudes. He was a pious man of singular honesty and fidelity—a strict observer of the Sabbath. New Mexico mountains were his final hunting range, and the charms of the Gila Wilderness held him to the end.

Like Lilly, I've lived my life as a hunter. Not with hounds, but with pencil and pad. It was never the ears of critters redeemed for bounty that kept me going. It was finding the truths of man. That and taking the whip from men's hands who set out to train a dog. In this regard, Lilly was maligned by the Ned Buntlines of his day.

Lilly lived his life in isolation, so when he hit the national press after President Theodore Roosevelt asked him to guide a bear hunt, the reporters concocted what they couldn't learn. One yarn begot another, until the man who made a science of ridding cattle killers from the range became the same man who would sentence a dog to death because he fouled up on the trail.

Well, Lilly knew lions and bears. But I know dog men. There was no way a man who lived his life in isolation, except for the companionship of his hounds, could brutalize the basis of his life. For not only were the hounds Lilly's only constant friends, they were the only way he could conduct his hunt. *Why then*, I asked myself, *would the hunter beat and kill his dogs*, any more than he would wrap his rifle barrel around a tree? It just didn't make sense, and I set out to prove it.

So grab your poke, fork your mount, and follow me. It's a cold trail before us, but as Milton once said in defense of freedom of the press, and I paraphrase, "Let truth and falsehood in an open field encounter. Who should have known truth to be bested on such a field of endeavor?"

First, the legend.

We saw it in Montauk Pilot, the Chesapeake Bay retriever; Jetstone Muscles of Claymar, a Lab; and John Law, an English pointer. A compulsion to get game no matter the obstructions, the hardships, the peril. Tidal waves, briar tangles, ice flows, even sheer rock walls were piddling nuisances that could not veer their quest, quench their fire, nor deter their hunt.

Then all this self-denying force appeared in an extraordinary man: Ben Lilly. If bears and mountain lions were truly man's enemy, as Ben Lilly became convinced they were, then he should have left the field of battle with fifty Congressional Medals of Honor ". . . for bravery and self-denial above and beyond the call of duty."

Theodore Roosevelt had Ben Lilly guide him on a bear hunt at Tensas Bayou, Louisiana, in 1907. The President wrote, "I never met a man so indifferent to fatigue and hardship. The morning he joined us in camp, he had come on foot through the thick woods, followed by his two dogs, and had neither eaten nor drunk for twenty-four hours: for he did not like to drink the swamp water. It had rained hard throughout the night and he had no shelter, no rubber coat, nothing but the clothes he was wearing, and the ground was too wet for him to lie on; so he perched in a crooked tree in the beating rain, much as if he had been a wild turkey."

Deprivation was Lilly's strength. He tried to hunt every day of his adult life and accomplished this goal between the ages of fifty-five and seventy. He entered the wilderness with no coat, no bedroll, no tent. The only food he carried was cornmeal, which he either ate as a gruel or baked into corn pone and shared with his hounds. He bedded down in the hide he just sliced from a bear or in the hollow of a fallen tree. He would set two logs afire and sleep between them or kick the embers from a fire trench (still hot) and sleep in the remaining warmth of the ground. He hunted every day of the year and glorified in feeling out track when it couldn't be sensed by man nor hound. He knew what bears and lions and dogs were going to do before they knew themselves. He once told a tag-along he felt sorry for any man who'd never been accepted into the family. For, he said, you can't live with them, and you can't hunt them if you aren't a member. The family, to Lilly, was the wilderness and the wild animals he hunted.

One evening Lilly killed a sow bear. He took her hide to sleep in only to be awakened by her mate trying to "get her attention." Lilly killed the male, too, and now he had a warm body to snuggle against as well as the warmth of the sow rug. Crawling one morning from a log where he'd spent the night, he started a fire; the warmth awakened a huge rattler, which then slithered out of the log. Lilly told the snake (for he talked to animals and said they talked to him; furthermore, he said he could look through man and animal: he could see their souls as X-rays saw their bones) he would spare the snake because he'd been spared. He shooed the rattler down the trail.

Lilly's strength was superhuman. He stood 5 feet 8 inches and weighed 180 pounds. Let me digress. When I hit the Lilly trail fifty years after his death, it is understandable that I generally met people who were either twenty to thirty years old or were children when they met him. All who knew Lilly when they were a child said he was 6 feet. That makes sense. Wouldn't you as a child, in the presence of a mountain man, see him 6 feet tall? But those who knew him as adults said he was 5 feet 6 inches to 5 feet 9 inches. I finally determined Lilly's true height visiting with Homer Pickens (lion hunter, 1930–35, and director of New Mexico Fish and Game, 1942–54), who stood and talked and walked and camped with Lilly for several years in the late 1920s and early 1930s.

Now back to Lilly's strength. He could, as a young man, reach out and grasp the snout of a 100-pound anvil and lift it with one hand (blacksmithing was one of his trades). He once came upon several men who'd killed a 400-pound bear and were trying to hoist it with a rope over a tree limb into their wagon. Lilly told them to get in the wagon bed and pull on the rope, then he picked up the bear, had them take in the slack, and snatch by snatch he got the bear loaded.

At fifty years of age, he could run without tiring ten miles at half-speed in pursuit of game. Earlier in life, he could stand flat-footed and jump out of a barrel. This is incredible. Try it! His backpacks, when he was carrying hides or supplies, generally ran between 50 and 150 pounds, and when asked, once, how he managed to carry so much, replied, "It's not the carrying that gets me. It's taking the thing off and feeling I'm just going to float away."

Lilly killed his first bear with a knife. No great feat, he said. If you always stab the bear on the side away from you, he'll jab his head that way. Just keep stabbing him on opposite sides, and he'll never have time to concentrate on you. The knife, incidentally, was homemade: Lilly used old files, horseshoer's rasps, or automobile springs for his steel, then tempered the blade in "panther" oil.

Lilly also carried, as a young man, a 22½-pound whip, tapered to thirty feet. Though he would not bet, he maintained a standing challenge that he could flick the open bottle caps from ten bottles of pop or beer without tipping a bottle. Think of the coordination. And it is said the earth-shattering crack of the whip could make a cow jump out of its skin. Think of the power.

Lilly always sought animals who could be his equal. Like keeping a pond of alligators in his youth: he would wrestle them in the evening when his chores were done.

His marksmanship became legendary. He claimed he never shot at anything he didn't hit. And he was competitive when young. He once took a stand with another shooter to harvest eighteen razorbacks. Lilly shot all eighteen, anticipating the next hog his co-shooter would aim for. Later, a Biological Survey trapper recalled Lilly shot a leaping lion three times, through vital spots, between the time it leaped and hit the ground.

Lilly entered the wilderness wearing five shirts; his pants legs were tied in ropes so nothing would snag. He always wore low-top shoes, which he heeled with burro shoes. After rubber tires became common, he would sole his shoes with sections of tread and a hundred hobnails. A rancher acquaintance said Lilly wore out regular shoe soles every two weeks. Once, while hunting grizzlies in northern Mexico, a writer came upon Lilly nailing deer skin on his shoe soles. He said to Lilly, "Aren't those nails a little long?" And he reported that Lilly told him,

"Yeah, but that keeps my feet from slipping around." A lady once weighed a pair of Lilly's tire-soled shoes: twelve pounds! Well-meaning friends would give Lilly a pair of boots, and he'd cut holes in the sides so the water could run out.

Though hard on self and what he called "varmints," Lilly was especially congenial to people (whom he seldom met) and flat doting on children, who loved his stories. True stories. Stories about treeing a bear and then sleeping with his feet inside the hollow trunk. When the bear tried to come down during the night (always backwards, as is their way), the bear would touch Lilly's foot and get kicked back up the tree until dawn when Lilly had light enough to shoot.

Traveling light—carrying only dog chains, a rifle, a homemade and lavishly scrimshawed hunting horn (Lilly was an accomplished outdoor artist), a pot, his sack of cornmeal, and his knife and Bible—Lilly nevertheless toted candy when he knew he'd be passing a ranch with children. He bought the candy by stopping a cowboy and writing a check either on the cowboy's cigarette paper or a chunk of aspen bark. He always signed his name with the picture of a bee for Ben, a stylized V for his middle initial, and a depiction of the lily flower for his last name. There was not a bank in the territory that would not honor the check for, surprisingly, Lilly had money in every one of them. He had, quite frankly, made a small fortune destroying cattle killers. The bounty was that high and he was that good. Later, the cowboy would catch up with Lilly and give him his store-bought candy and some cinnamon sticks (the latter being the man's only luxury).

But whoa there, Nelly, I'm having a runaway. I'm not vindicating Lilly. It's that way when I get to puttin' the ink on Lilly. And that's why a kernel of truth about the man so often became a stalk of corn in the hands of eager reporters: even one college professor. They ended up, if you will pardon the expression, "Gilding the Lilly."

The sensationalist reporting about Lilly was crystallized by the leading folklorist of his day, J. Frank Dobie, a Texas professor, Guggen-heim fellow, and visiting lecturer to Cambridge University in England, who asks us to believe on pages 171–72 in his best-selling book, *The Ben Lilly Legend* (Little, Brown and Co., 1950), that "He [Lilly] was very jealous of the Lilly string [of hunting dogs]. During his big years as a hunter in the West, he would not sell a male without castrating him or a bitch without spaying her.

"If Lilly got hold of a dog irresponsive to training, he would kill it. He would not give away a dog to be pampered in town. He thought that dogs had a right, like himself, to follow the instinct for hunting. A dog without that instinct was to him a betrayer of the species. If, after he had trained a dog, it persisted in quitting the trail of a lion or bear for something else . . . he would call his dogs around him as witnesses, explain to them very definitely the crime of interfering with the work of top dogs and call upon them as fellow hunters to see justice in the death penalty. He would talk to the guilty one sternly but without anger, and then either beat him to death or shoot him."

Subsequent writers who would research Lilly, too often researched Dobie instead. So the legend of the hunter who would kill his dogs came down through the decades without questioning.

For example, writing in *La Ventura* magazine, supplement to the *Silver City Daily Press*, on December 7, 1968, Allton Turner picks up the same theme when he writes, "If a dog refused to mind or just could-n't be trained, Mr. Lilly disposed of him."

Though editors and readers alike let such allegations go unchal-lenged, they just didn't set right with me. They rang untrue and un-natural. They rang so hard they became the bell that put me in the fight. Yet I can see why such statements were accepted. We need to un-derstand the time in which Lilly lived. He was born in 1856, came to manhood in 1868 (that's when he first left home), and was hunting nearly full-time by 1876. These were times when men could be rough on their dogs, as we'll see below, but that doesn't necessarily extend to being brutal to them. These were not the days of sportsmen. To the hunter, it meant get or be got; to the rancher, get or be had—for varmints would kill their stock. There was no forty-hour week, no Occupational Safety and Health Administration, no game laws in most parts, no veterinarians, no SPCA, and no Walt Disney with Bambi.

Even as late as 1935, Hemingway wrote on safari in *Green Hills of Africa*, ". . . but the greatest joke of all . . . was the hyena, the classic hyena, that hit too far back while running, would circle madly, snapping and tearing at himself until he pulled his own intestines out, and then stood there, jerking them out and eating them with relish."

Humane hunting, conservation, and an ethic regarding all life had to wait until now.

Yet, I can't group Lilly with practitioners of inhumanity to life. I know dog men. And like Robert Frost wrote in his poem, "Two Tramps in Mud Time" (and I paraphrase), "Except as a man handles their tool, they have no way of judging a fool." Lilly handled my tool: gun dogs. And intuitively I knew he was not guilty as charged. So fifty years after the fact, I hit the trail to clear him of this injustice. This is what I found.

My guide was Jim Essick, city librarian of Silver City, New Mexico (I have ridden with no better hunter), who pointed me as follows.

Mrs. Lillian Leonard, of Silver City (Lilly hunted north of this town the last twenty years of his life in the 750,000-acre Gila wilderness area), remembered her father-in-law had a sawmill at Pinos Altos (a former gold-mining town) up on the Black Range. Her husband, Bob, worked for his dad. And Lillian was left to tend the commissary: a company store where lumberjacks would buy overalls, boots, and tobacco.

Lilly came to the commissary door one day asking for her husband. He said, "I've got a dog that has to be put down, and I can't do it. I wonder if Bob would do it for me?"

Now, I've doubled on passing geese and come within twelve pounds of a world record on *dorrado* (the dolphinfish of the Sea of Cortez), but those thrills pale to the one I felt when I heard this one declarative sentence from a simple inquiry. Ben Lilly laid himself bare to what he was. A man who loved his dogs. This dog was doomed: he may have stepped in a trap, got mauled by a bear, or come down with distemper. Who knows? But Lilly couldn't put him away. By his very nature he had to ask another. So much for Lilly the dog killer.

Now, let's stop a moment and savor this one find. The truth becomes so simple you have to wonder how anyone got by with deception. Ready for more? Let's go.

Tracey Neal of Central, New Mexico, was driving up Cherry Creek Road one Sunday when Ben Lilly stepped from the woods, waving him down. Lilly approached the car and asked, "Would you shoot a mountain lion in a trap for me? It's Sunday and I can't do it."

Let's put this in perspective. Mountain lion and bear were killing 20 percent of the southeastern Arizona and southwestern New Mexico ranchers' cattle and other livestock. The ranchers petitioned the government to save their livelihood. Ben Lilly was paid by the U. S. Biological Survey (forerunner of today's U. S. Fish and Wildlife Service) to aid the cattlemen. He also was given bonuses by these same ranchers to rid them of their cattle killers. Extermination was Lilly's job, but not inhumanity. Here he had a lion in a trap but couldn't stand to see it suffer until Monday morning when his iron-clad steadfastness to the Bible would let him put the animal out of its misery. So he asked another.

Lilly lived in a rigid framework of Christianity and ethics. There are things you do and things you don't. Lilly never got confused between the two. Life and suffering meant something to him. And if he could not see his prey suffer, how could he inflict pain on his hounds? The answer is evident to me: he couldn't.

I asked Tracey Neal, "Was Lilly mean to his dogs?"

The retired Forest Service employee said in almost defiant voice, "He slept with them, didn't he?"

Ralph Dinwiddie, of Silver City, lived at Cliff, New Mexico, with his father, who owned a large store. Lilly would sometimes camp in the yard during the summer when he'd buy supplies. I asked Dinwiddie if he ever saw Lilly with a whip. That would be the thing to strike a dog with. Dinwiddie said, "Yes, he did carry the thing. But I never knew what for. I never saw him use it."

I do not imply Lilly pampered his pack. Why should he? He sure didn't pamper himself. Dinwiddie recalled, "One time my father was camping and hunting over on Turkey Creek, which is a very rugged wilderness area, and Ben Lilly had bedded down outside his camp. Come morning, my father told me, Lilly woke up and waded across the creek with ice all over it and went on up the hill like nothing happened." It stands to reason a dog was expected to meet life with equal indifference—but I suspicion no more than the man he hunted with.

Lilly didn't have the capability either to see or avoid hardship. His dogs were expected to be equally blind.

But the man who nailed it all down for me was Homer Pickens, former mountain lion hunter and retired director for the New Mexico Fish and Game Department. He told me from his Albuquerque home, "I had a lot of respect for Mr. Lilly and was close to him the last years of his life. Any insinuation of Mr. Lilly being cruel to his dogs was wrong, definitely wrong. And as for neutering an animal before selling it, that is definitely wrong. Mr. Lilly just wasn't of that nature."

So there it was. I did what I set out to do. Ben Lilly was exonerated of all hack-journalism charges that he was brutal to his string, a wilderness judge who sentenced slack dogs to die, and a man with a knife who'd cut the cords before letting a dog fall into someone else's hands. It was all bosh. And then I recalled two stories that support my thinking.

In a rare written account left by Lilly, he tells of tracking a grizzly on the Blue River in Arizona. "I followed him for three days," Lilly wrote, "and during that time I did not have one mouthful to eat." The snow was deep, and Lilly was wearing a pair of cotton pants, a work shirt, and a light cotton sweater. When he finally killed the bear, Lilly wrote, "I felt weak. My dogs and I both needed water. There was some under ice not far away, and we started to it. On the way we struck a lion track, very fresh. I felt like a new man and took out in a run." Lilly killed the lion and wrote, "After I skinned him, the dogs and I had a good meal. I wrapped up in the skin by the carcass and slept as warm as if I were in a stove."

For a gun dog to live like this is not abuse: it's rapture. If Lilly had struck a second mountain lion track, the dogs would have wanted to tree that one before they ate the first one. For some men and all-class gun dogs there is something maniacally sublime in the hunt.

A Mimbres River writer and adventurer, M. H. "Dutch" Salmon, once talked to a Gila wilderness rancher named Jack Hooker about Ben Lilly. Most backwoods people who knew Lilly were aware that his favorite camp was in a cave on Sapillo Creek. Hooker also knew that Lilly buried something in front of that cave. After Lilly died, Hooker started wondering what could have been so precious for Lilly to dig a hole.

He told Salmon, "I went up there and dug it up. Could it be a knife, maybe some money? But you know what it was? It was the grave of one of Lilly's best hounds. He buried Crook there, and on a shoe box in pencil wrote this out."

Hooker handed out the box lid and Salmon read, in what he told me was longhand more elegant than grammatical, "Here lies Crook a bear and lion dog that helped kill 210 bear and 426 mountain lion since 1914 owned by B. V. Lilly. He died here the first Tuesday night in February 1925. He was owned and raised in camp and died in camp here. B. V. Lilly, February 1925."

So I rest my case. *Lilly loved the dogs with whom he lived his life.* Maligned by a national press that laughed behind his back at his "quaintness," Lilly became my idol. But he was a fallen idol. I set about to right him. And though I arrived at the eleventh hour, there were enough people still living who knew Lilly to get the job done, to set the record straight.

To all the above-cited goes my gratitude. But there were, in addition, Tod Wilson, Hough Hodge, Orval Little, and Mrs. Terry Tipton, all of Silver City, and Glen Lilly, of Mesa, Arizona.

To all of them I say, "Ben Lilly and I thank you."

8

OF MIRACLES AND MEMORIES

I *bought Wasatch Renegade and Uneva Drake's Lucky Lady when they were ten years old or more because they had once thrown two field champions out of the same litter. I was hoping these Labs could do it again. They never did, and it was many years later that Bob Wehle, of Midway, Alabama, the world's top gun dog breeder, gave me insight into what happened. He told me he learned that producing males should be under a year old to throw great beget. He now knew, he said, the younger the better.*

Well anyway, I had many great gun dogs in their prime at that time, but on occasion I'd take Rene or Toughie, as the dam was called, to the duck blind.

It was a cold and iced-over late November dawn when Rene and I made the hunt. That afternoon I wrote what follows.

Old gun dogs have stood the test of time and event and circumstance. They come now, slowly, and lay at foot or close to side, jowls flat, eyes faded with the fog of cataract, their muzzles and paws white or speckled salt and pepper. But they come. They want to be close.

They are great treasures, these old dogs. Lying there, they are more than themselves. They are us. Parts of us. A hill climbed together and the crimson leaves of sumac danced in the morning sunlight. The well looked in and the rock dropped; the chill of the dark hole seemed to go on forever before the splash was heard.

They are sweaty palms, for you were hosting your boss and he'd never gunned over a trained dog before. But Pup was so birdy you couldn't be sure he'd hold for shot and wing.

They are the iced mace of wind thrown by bad-dad winter, off to the north, blowing the red-leg mallards off their winter haunts. Blowing them south, flying like buckshot. And you're gripping Pup and whispering, "No head up," as you fit the duck call to your lips. It is so cold you know it will freeze to the skin. But you call. And the lead hen throws her body high, looking down and back, seeing the iced-in blocks pointing bill-up to the slate sky.

And now they come, shingles ripped loose from some old barn. The wind is driving them crazily toward your decoys, and you stand and the old gun barks and the dog launches. He's breaking ice and standing high in the water, though his feet don't touch bottom. And you wish you'd never shot. For nothing can live out there—not even Pup in the prime of his life. Yet he clomps the big bright drake and spins about, throwing water with his whipping tail. He comes for you—the drake covering his face—swimming by instinct, for he cannot see.

You're out of the blind now and running the bank, yelling out. The retriever comes to shore, not stopping to shake, and heads straight for you. But the black dog turns instantly silver. The water has frozen that fast. You take the duck and the dog shivers, his teeth chattering, and the pelvic-drive muscles convulse. Then he spins in the tall yellow grass: he runs and rubs the side of his jowls in the mud and stubble.

No duck is worth this—remember saying that?—and the two of you go back to the house. Back to the towel you rub over Pup and the fire you sit before as the wind makes a harmonica of your house-siding and whomps down the fireplace to billow the ashes.

But the duck does lay on the sideboard by the sink. You entered nature, went duck hunting, tricked the wildfowl to your trap, and the dog closed the door.

Still, you're sorry you went; but years later, when the smell of that day's wet fur is forgotten and the curled tail feathers from the mallard have long been blown from the fireplace mantle, you'll remember that retrieve and old Pup will come to side. You'll fondle his ears and the memory of that cold day and that single duck will become the most important thing that ever happened in your life.

For Pup is dying.

You can't see him, but you have to smile and call him to you. It may be the last time you ever touch his ear. But that's just part of it. You're dying, too (we all are, you know). Pup just will go first. As he always went first in the field and at the blind. You followed him, not the other way around. It was he who entered the unknown and learned its bareness or its bounty.

You love the old dog, for he lived your life. He was the calendar of your joy. Why, you could leap the stream when you got your first pup. Remember? And you could hunt all day. Cold? Bosh! And the apple in your pocket was all it took to fuel you from Perkin's fence to Hadley's barn—a limit of bobwhite later.

But now the arthritis hobbles you. And the cold. It seems to come and sit in your bones like an unwanted stranger.

So you don't just call Pup to side, you call your life. You run your fingers through your past when you fondle his ears.

You stand and go to the gun case. Why, the bluing's gone from that old Superposed. Then you remember when you bought it: long before Pup ever came into your life. And look at that duck call. There's no varnish left on the barrel. And the barrel is cracked! And the string that holds it. It was a country store back in the hills; you stopped for hamburger to feed Pup. And the duck call was in your pocket, just out of its cardboard box. You asked the proprietor for a piece of string and he went to the meat counter and drew off a yard of it. You were always going to get a bona fide, braided lanyard.

But that's like life. You were always going to. . . .

And there's Pup. He was not a going to. He was a was. Not a put-off till tomorrow. Pup was planned and bought and trained and taken to field. That happened. And the million dollars was never made, and you never became branch manager, and your kids didn't make it through college. But Pup did all you imagined for him.

Pup was your one success.

And he is dying.

How many pups ago was it your sweater fitted loose on your belly, and your belly was hard like the barrel of a cannon? But look at the sweater now. Stretched tight and tattered and faded. Why do you still wear it? There are Christmas sweaters still in their boxes on the shelf in the closet.

And the boots. Remember? They had to be just so. But look at them now. Toes out, scuffed, heels run over. And yet you shuffle about in them.

Is it because you're holding on to the past? Is it because looking back down the road means more than looking on up ahead? Is it because the birds you went with Pup to get were got? And now? What do they say? A bird in the hand is worth more than two—maybe that's it.

Pup made you a bird-in-the-hand man.

Others, in those days, may have been two-bird hopefuls. But you and Pup did it. You went. No sunshine patriots then. No sir. That bird was in hand.

He's got bad teeth now, you know? Pup has. And let's admit it: his breath stinks. And look at him, great blotches of hair hang here and there like some derelict mountain sheep that's taken to roadside begging. And he does little but sleep—and pass gas. He does lots of that.

There are pups to be bought, you know? Why, ads are everywhere. And some say gun dogs have gotten better than ever. Or at least the training methods have gotten so sharp you can even bring a mediocre pup along.

But no. It's always been you and Pup. And you'll wait till he's no more. But have you ever wondered? What will you be when he's gone?

If he was the best part of your days, then what will there be when he's dead and buried? What will there be of you? Some grumpy old mumbler who sits by the fire and harrumphs at those who come to be kind?

No, not at all. For you were a gun dog man and you went to field. Your Pup was the best gun dog you ever saw. And you watched the flash of the great black dog as he leaped through bramble and you saw him once atop the hill. How far away was he on that cast? A half mile! And all you must do is close your eyes; better yet, just go to the window and watch the falling leaves. Pup's out there. He's by the gate. See him? And he's leaping that way he always did, urging you to get on with it. And he darts now, to the field, and sniffs the passing mice, the dickey birds.

And then you're with him, the weight of the gun reassuring in your grasp. Your stride is strong and the wind bites your cheek, but you laugh and blow the white steam of cold. Always you can do this, just standing at the window—for you did this.

What of the smell of straw at the old duck blind and pouring the coffee from the Thermos. Then learning how to pour the coffee from the steel cup so you could put the cup to your lips. And you never knew why the pouring made the cup manageable.

And the pride in your homemade decoys, watching them run to the end of their cords and spin about, ducking their heads and bobbing to drip water from their bills.

And off to the left, in that stand of multiflora rose: Hear him! The cock pheasant *car-runks*. Bright as brass he is. And you could heel Pup out of the duck blind and go get him, but you like his sass. You like his arrogance. And the fact that anything that gaudy can live out there in the back of your place.

And what of the morning you and Pup were sitting there? Duck hunting for you didn't mean shooting ducks. It meant being there. Hearing the russle of your heavy canvas pants and the tinkle of the dog whistles and calls as they danced on your chest. Blowing in cupped hands, beating them against the sides of your chest. And standing and stomping on the wood pallets you brought in because the water rose with the late rains. And for that moment you and Pup were silent and the redtailed hawk landed, right above both of you, on a naked limb.

You were ornery. Jumped up, you did, and yelled, "Hey, Hawk!" And the hawk was so discombobulated he hurled himself to the air with a great squawk, leaving a white stream all over your blind as he beat his departure. But it was still funny, and you sat in the draping of hawk feces—and laughed.

Not another single living thing had that moment but you and Pup and the hawk. And the three of you made that moment momentous forever. The hawk is gone and Pup is going but that moment makes you all vibrant and alive. And in a way it makes you important. Who else ever had an exclusive moment?

And if Pup had not taken you to field, you'd not have had it. So he lays there now, that generator of meaning and memory. That's what a

gun dog comes to be for us. An enricher of life. Something to take or-
dinary moments and make them miraculous.

That's why the love for Pup is so great. What matter if he passes
gas and has bad breath and moans in his sleep. He's earned his trans-
gressions. And he tells us of our own end. For sharing the best with
him, we must now share the worst with him, and we lie there, too.

But dog men push that away. Their Pup was a springer spaniel, you
know. Oh, how happy he was afield. Why the stub of his tail couldn't
be tallied as it wagged. And it wagged that way when idle or working.
He was just that happy. And he made the man happy. For happiness is
infectious, and there's no known cure. Not even disaster. For you'll
walk around the knowledge of disaster to peek in memory at that happy
tail.

And that man's Pup was a beagle. A mellow-voiced ground snorter
if ever there was one. The bow legs, all that massed muscle. And how
he used to launch the rabbit and then dart out in pursuit, giving the
man instructions—Loud Instructions!—on when to shoot.

But that's not the Pup I was thinking of. No. That Pup was your
cocker with thick hair the color of wheat tassels; he'd rut to launch the
bird, down in the mud, going under the high-water log. And up he'd
come with that smashed face, little mud balls hanging from his silver
whiskers, and in a turn—which was more like a complete flip—he'd tell
you with his body signal there was nothing down there and you'd best
be off.

But who am I to talk like this? You know your Pup better than I
ever could. For there was just the two of you—oh, maybe a hawk! And
what happened can never happen again. No man and dog could ever be
that rich, that lucky, that blessed again.

Yet, each year several million new pups are taken into American
homes, into American hearts. All on the knowledge that there are some
miracles and memories left out there yet.

GRAND JUNCTION: BIRD DOG
CAPITAL OF THE WORLD

Except for a Kansas farm where I once lived, Grand Junction, Tennessee, has spurred me to write more stories than any other place on earth. Maybe it's because my friend Wilson Dunn lives there; not a year goes by that I don't visit him. Or maybe it's the Junction Inn, one of those blue-plate diners by the railroad tracks where you can get a catfish fillet platter that melts in your mouth. Or maybe it's the good people who live there. Or because every immortal bird dog man America ever produced came there and competed there and did all those things that put him in the Hall of Fame. And I'll be damned if the Hall doesn't stand there, too.

6 5

It all began in these parts, you know, many a wet moon ago. For it takes a place where the moon stays wet to grow the weed that makes the seed to feed the bird that calls the man to cast his dog—to have a go.

Grand Junction, Tennessee! Four hundred people now, never any more. Five inches of rain a month, long as anyone can recall. A place where two rail lines cross. And the name? Well, if you have no more than that, yet you'd like to be more than what you seem to be—then you call the place Grand Junction. So that's how the place was named: for doubtful railroad fame.

Ironically, this place really is a Grand Junction. For reasons you will see.

I walk the vacant street tonight, the wet moon walled behind thick clouds, which now and then grow thin so the moon shines through and the night sky colors to pewter. Off to the northwest a train whistles three times. The call comes searchingly on the damp air: melancholy and haunting, like a cold-trailing hound way off yonder making game in a hollow.

I stop. There's the junction, and I see in my mind's eye Mr. Hobart Ames' private railroad car—just down from Boston—parked on the siding. (Modern journalism never uses the title, Mister, but I've never heard Mr. Ames called any other way.)

Let's back up. In 1774 Mr. Ames' great-great (add or subtract a great, I really don't know) granddaddy pushed a wheelbarrow of shovels into Braintree, Massachusetts. He asked a dime apiece in a five-cent market and the people said, "No." Old man Ames got mad, threw the shovels to the ground, and left. But when he came back later to sell more ten-cent shovels, the public had used those he abandoned and judged them to be worth the nickel more. Thus the birth of the Ames Tool Company.

Now, let's step to side for a second. Fifty-nine miles due east of where I stand tonight, a two-day battle ended with 23,741 American casualties. The dates: April 6 and 7, 1862. The place: Shiloh, named for a little white wooden church that stood there. And ninety years after the shovel success, another Ames is building (among other hardware) a cannon. These cannons fired for the Union Army at Shiloh. And General Grant writes that he can walk across a field and never touch the ground with his boot soles (actually, he was on a horse). There are that many dead Confederates to walk on. Soldiers, who at the end, charged the face of the cannons with only their fixed bayonets. The Rebs were out of ammunition.

Thirty-five years later this Mr. Hobart Ames (with the private railroad car from Boston) of Braintree shovel and Shiloh cannon fame (the cannon that planted thousands of Confederates on a battlefield fifty-nine miles any) comes to buy a plantation that will grow to 16,800 acres—and no one will ever mention the cannon.

Now that's amazing, ain't it? The cannons fired in 1862, the railroad car is parked in 1901; that's only thirty-nine years, and no one says a word. Matter of fact, it will take another eighty years before anyone mentions the cannon. I just did.

And you know that other people stood where I'm standing tonight and looked at that railroad car and thought of their father, brother, son, husband, cousin, nephew, or friend who died at Shiloh. They know of the cannon. Heck, this is Tennessee, and Mississippi is only four miles away. That's a mighty great blood grudge to lay aside, don't you think? For as one private monument erected at Shiloh reads, "Three generations of Remberts. To my dear parents and loving sisters and my noble, gentle, brilliant and brave brother, killed for defending home against the most devious lot of cut throats that ever cursed the face of this earth."

Well, it's a strange thing about men. They'll kill each other in battle, pull a slick deal and bankrupt each other, and run away with each other's wives; but let the bobwhite call, and the pointers leap against their collars, and suddenly most men are brothers. The brotherhood of huntin', the most ennobling undertaking God ever gave to man.

The first field trial ever run in this country occurred on the old Greenlaw Plantation now in the eastern suburbs of Memphis, Tennessee. That was 1874. Just twelve years after Shiloh—and the Yankees were there. And welcomed there. Yet, get this. As late as 1890, when the federal government built the visitor's center at Shiloh, they flat refused ". . . to have any improvement, the cemetery, or anything, on ground that had been lost to the Confederates in the Battle of Shiloh by the Union Army." This quote's from Terry Smith, one of the blind fools, who for many years was a tour guide at Shiloh.

Because of Terry's revelation, we now know why the Shiloh park starts at the back instead of the front where it should. And we learn that even today (I wrote this piece in 1981) the Confederate dead at Shiloh are still mass-buried in trenches. The Union soldiers were all interred individually in 1866. Vengeance is mine, sayeth the North!

It's just flat evident, no need to say more, that the greatest truce maker in the world is a gun dog and a bird.

Now, let me get all this in order for you. On a rainy night I'm standing in Grand Junction, and Grand Junction it is: not for railroad fame, but for gun dogs. A crow's flight 100 miles south by southeast will put you over West Point, Mississippi, where the first National Bird Dog Championship trial was ever held in America: February 10 and 11, 1896. The winner: an English setter named Count Gladstone IV, a white, black, and tan Llewellyn owned by F. R. Hitchcock and whelped by breeder Charles Tucker on October 29, 1889.

In 1897, 1898, and 1899, the national field trial committee will move up and down the Kansas City, Fort Scott, and Memphis Railroad looking for suitable grounds. One year it is too cold (17 above), another year a poor bird crop, and still another year the town comes down with a smallpox epidemic.

So in 1900, the national committee asks the United States Field Trial Club—which was just concluding its trial two miles south of Grand Junction—if the National Championship could dovetail the conclusion of the U.S. trial and run on these same grounds. The answer is, "Yes."

Then, except for two runnings at Hickory Valley, Tennessee (just up the road apiece), the national will be run forevermore at Grand Junction. First to the south, then to the north, then to the south— when Mr. Hobart Ames arrives from Boston, buys the old John Walker Jones "Cedar Grove" Plantation just northeast of Grand Junction and invites the nation to run on his property in 1902. The national's fate and site is sealed. And, through a trust established by Mr. Hobart Ames upon his death, the Ames Plantation will remain the permanent home of the National Championship.

Now, why did Ames come to Grand Junction? Well, he was a bird hunter who was looking for birdy land. While nosing around New Albany, Mississippi, Jim Avent (the Fox of Hickory Valley—a many-time national winner and a notorious suspect for cheating at trials) invited Ames to see the Jones place. Ames did, forfeited earnest money left in Mississippi, and took possession of Cedar Groves.

So, who is this Avent? Well, all the men I mention here, all these men who made Grand Junction the crossroads of world gun dogdom, are giants. Just giants. Jim Avent was a gentleman and scoundrel (according to Herman Jenkins whose occupation is logging each day's weather in Grand Junction), a sportsman and a scalawag (according to Mrs. Clyde Raines who runs the local hotel), and a wealthy man and a pauper (just depended on when you met him) who owned four dogs that won the national title five times, handled seven dogs to eight national titles, and bred five dogs that won the title six times. This same man, Jim Avent, also knifed a man to death in broad daylight (according to Buck Park, an aged bird dog handler) on the main street of Hickory Valley when the stranger kicked one of Avent's dogs.

Once wealthy enough to lease a railroad car to carry his January/February house guests to the seven trials run each year at Grand Junction, Avent concluded his life in reduced circumstances, taking his meals with his fellow handlers at the Raines Hotel. Millionaire sportsman Paul Rainey (whom we'll meet later on) paid the tab and told Mrs. Raines not to say a word about it to Avent: America's first super-star of dogdom.

And this is interesting. The Jones who built the plantation Ames bought—well, that Jones was the great-grandfather of Irma Jones who married Nash Buckingham in 1910. And if I have to tell you who Nash Buckingham was, I'd also have to tell a graduating university class of political scientists about a man named Lincoln.

It just fascinates me. The way great men and great places and great deeds always seem to form circles within circles—without end. All this history, all these giants, all within 100 miles in any direction from Grand Junction.

Like Herman Jenkins. He's eighty-three the year I write this piece; he won the national "amatoor," as he says it in 1923, and was field trial marshall for the national open for twenty years.

Just north and a block east of Herman's place is Mrs. Clyde Raines hotel. This is where the drawing for the running of the national took place for decades, and most of the owners and handlers stayed here one time or another. Mrs. Raines spends an afternoon with me, sitting in her sun-splashed parlor, the aluminum walker near her left hand. But her voice is full, her mind as sharp as a coon evading a pack of hounds, and her summary of guests outspoken. Mrs. Raines is eighty-six, and as she says it, "I fed 'em and slept 'em from 1919 to 1974."

Then there's the dandy, Buck Park. He was Mrs. Julia Colony

Ames' choice as the "best" of all the hangers-on who bird-dogged the Ames place. Mrs. Ames was Mr. Ames' widow, and she made certain the rules within his will were carried out. Buck Park was the sidekick of financial barons, a slick who could draw an inside straight, the ride-'em-to-sweat bird dog handler who yelled instructions at his competitors and got them to listen. Buck Park is in a nursing home near Grand Junction when I visit him. How old is Buck? I forgot to ask.

And Wilson Dunn is here. He's only sixty-three when I write this, which makes him a rookie hereabouts (he will win the national in 1990). Wilson came here years ago to sell calico skirts to the plantation women and hoes to the wage farmers. But always a runner of dogs, Wilson was. Why he was born just up the road a few miles. Then Wilson gradually turns his general store into a gun dog supply house that now grosses some three million dollars a year selling dog collars, horse blankets, and camo shirts to outdoorsmen.

My point in recounting all this is simple: all these people, all of this enterprise, all this history, all this portent for tomorrow is here at Grand Junction for just one reason. A little bird. That's what this place and this article is all about. A little brown-and-white bird that brought all these people to this place. To park railroad cars, to buy plantations, to forgive a Civil War, to write immortal prose (remember Nash Buckingham), to knock a hole in the horizon in trail of an old pointer's tail. To go bird hunting.

We say the dove is the bird of peace.

Maybe.

I'd say, though, the bobwhite quail is the bird of peace and prosperity and posterity.

And I'd also say this. Webster tells us a sportsman, ". . . is one who is fair and generous and a good loser and a graceful winner." Though the average Southerner might not be able to forgive a Yankee, and the average Yankee not be able to forgive a Reb, the outdoor sportsmen of each locale had no alternative—lest he forfeit his very being.

And there is this to know and to remember. The Ames family was making weaponry in Massachusetts before the War of 1812. And all sportsman know it is not the gun that kills people, it is people who kill people. Like the single Ames cannon still on display at Shiloh. It started the day in the hands of the Union, but was captured by the Confederacy and used against it's previous owners. Then it was hauled to Corinth, Mississippi, where it was lost back to the 1st U. S. Infantry of the Union Army in October at the Battle of Corinth.

In the hands of soldiers, the cannon killed the enemy. When no soldier was there to fire it, it was silent.

As this cannon has been for more than 100 years.

Now that the Field Trial Hall of Fame has its permanent quarters in Grand Junction, visit there. See all the immortal men and dogs for yourself. And don't forget to listen for the train's mournful whistle and to order something fit to eat at the nearby Junction café.

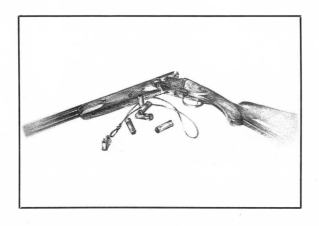

10

A Greater Hunter

I've seldom met a gun dog man who didn't have a buddy—and I'm not thinking of his dog. It's a man. A rare man, a good man, an accomplished man, a selfless man.

A man who'll go hunting with you even if it's his daughter's wedding day. For me, that man is Jim Culbertson of Wichita, Kansas. And speaking of weddings . . .

I remember the time Doctor Robert Moore's daughter was getting married in Hoisington, Kansas (their home), just next to that bonanza waterfowl mecca called Cheyenne Bottoms. Jim and I were invited to the wedding, but that meant giving up the dusk shooting of green-wing teal that were pouring into a flooded field of weed seed.

Never mind. Jim and I caught the bride coming from the church; we threw our rice dressed in camo coats and rubber waders.

Say hello to Jim!

It's opening day on bobwhite, and we're outside Buffalo, Kansas. It's a very important place, for Buffalo advertises itself as "The Hedgepost Capital of the World."

Jim stops the pickup. It's dark on the dirt road, but off to the east an overcast sky shows that grime of weathered aluminum. I slide from the truck's seat, clear my throat, feel the chat on boot soles. There is a bite to the morning's cold.

Grappling behind the seat, I dig the imitation leather gun case from the debris. Sliding it forward, my hands touch the familiar strips of silver duct tape that seal the holes where the case has ripped. I slide the shotgun from the old case. There are the deep gouges left by barbed wire in the stock: I use it to bend down the wire my short legs never quite manage to clear. The smell of cleaning fluid and gun oil coils faintly in the air. I touch the steel of the barrel. It is slick, cold perfection.

But the Labs will have none of my dawdling. (Yes, Jim and I always hunt bobwhite with Labs.) They rock their crates and I sense the fast breathing and slobber of them. Hurrying around in back of the pickup bed, I drop the tailgate and spring the crate latches: I jerk away fast so the flung-back doors won't catch me as the dogs launch, carrying themselves high with arched backs. Away from the truck they fling themselves, running now in circles, noses down, twirling, dumping, scraping back as they continue to run, barging into the brittle weeds of the ditch.

I mumble to Jim, "It's all here as we left it."

He ignores my philosophy and yells into the dawn, "It's opening day, Willy Boy."

I tell him, "But there has been no time between last season's last day and this season's first day. Fall of '85 bumps into winter of '84 as simply and smoothly as shells into a gun."

Jim says, "S'cuse me," as he grabs for his canvas ammo pouch.

I will make my point. I say, "There never was a summer, there never was that time when the gun was empty."

Jim grunts and leaps the borrow ditch. He's leaving.

I finger the shells midst the lint and cracker crumbs and weed seed in my coat pocket. I never keep the pocket flaps out and over like I'm supposed to. The flap always curls and sticks up for fast, but often futile, grabs at shells. It is a matter of fumbling, then finally seating the shells. Lifting the gun as the flutter of wings is heard. Blowing bark off the trees to the wind.

It all comes back now. I tell myself, *Hunting is sensing. The way the sun comes up on cold mornings that orange of a branding iron. Melting the ice from the bent-backed grass. The tough, yellow prairie grass that'll slice your hand if you swipe through it real fast.*

Then I suddenly know; *"Hunting is never quite believable. Take the color of fall sumac! Or the way the sun shines in the yellow cottonwood leaves as though each leaf had a lightbulb in it.*

Jim yells back, through the brush, "There's a cardinal . . ." I hear him barging on. He adds, "There's bound to be a covey of quail within a hundred yards of a cardinal, huh?"

I don't answer him, but watch instead as the Labs run onto the pond. The thing is iced. They slide there, puzzled but a moment as they scrape about and leave. They would have had a drink. But it all comes back to them, too. For they run the bank about the pond and top the dam, going over to drink from the spillway where they'll lap at the silver water.

It is smelling the treasure of old scent, I tell myself. *From years of it soaked through the armpits of this old hunting coat and down the back and around the grimed neck. A smell near that of horse harness. A hunter never buys new clothes: I don't anyway. I sense it would be some sort of defeat. Old clothes are like a crutch or a bandage to distinguish a real veteran of the battle.*

I have this damnable habit. I can't walk without humming. Each step is a note, and suddenly I realize I'm bushed: winded. And, sure enough, up come the birds. Me and my hum of the *Battle Hymn of the Republic* and there they are. They ambush me in explosion. And I suck the cold air deep and jerk the gun up; the gray smoke lifts back and a curl of it comes to my nose like snuff to the gums. I wish I had some snuff. But I gave it up. My adult life has been a series of giving things up.

The dogs search in vain for the birds I didn't shoot and I say nothing. Rather, I watch the live birds down and take resolve as I seat new shells to wait the next rise. To not shoot the sky, but to wait. To not shoot at the covey, but to think. To shoot at a single, solitary bird. Not a flock! A bird!

My boots slide back in the mud of the creek bank as I huff to the rim and see him standing there, see him laughing. His laugh is always a taunt. Jim always gets a bird. So I never ask him how he did. When he invites me to dinner next week, the birds on my plate will have shot in them. That's the way Jim tells me he got a bird. That is the way Jim tells me (at his kitchen table) he got all the birds.

But how does he do it? That's the question. And that's the value. Why, that's the crux of the whole matter. Oh, I don't mean like here at the creek with him standing there with that silly grin on his face. I mean like usual. You know, he's into the covey rise and his model 12 sounds automatic. And why am I not firing? Because Jim kicked up the birds while *I was a straddle the fence*. He always does that.

Or, the dogs are making game and I'm digging in, assuring myself I'll not fail this time, telling myself everything will be all right, when Jim does two things at the same time. He raises his Model 12 with his right arm and knocks me sideways with his left elbow, blurting, "Oh, I'm sorry there . . . I slipped." And his gun is smoking. And I'm still flying sideways; Jim was an All-American football guard and knocking people sideways was what he did best. And even though his power is now old, it is still power.

Or, there are the popper shells he secrets into my gun. Those pel-letless shells used at field trials. So I fire blanks. Or there have been nights Jim's taken a split shot—like those you fish with—and crimped it to a sting and wadded the string into an empty shell. And when I fired the next morning, the string spiraled out, looking silver in the bright sunlight, looking endless. And Jim is shouting at me as he goes to his knees in the tall, yellow grass. He yells,"Willy Boy . . . you've shot the lining out of your damned barrel. The whole cotton-pickin' lining . . ."

Yes, Jim secrets all manner of things into my gun. Would you be-lieve little plastic salt-and-pepper shakers sold at sporting goods stores that look like shells?

What about duck feathers? What about them, huh? He stuffs the empty shells with duck feathers and never lets me fire until I'm down-wind. I should know. When did Jim ever give me a shot? When the big mallard comes in, and Jim in conspiratorial voice says, "Take him Willy Boy . . ." I fire; the feathers blast from the gun, washing back with the wind, covering my face, my clothes. I spit at them and swipe at them, and Jim's telling me, seriously, "You got him Willy Boy. Why, he's fly-ing naked. Dressed in the sky . . . flat dressed out in the sky."

The wind turns colder now. That's the way with Kansas. It never did have a thermostat that worked. And the cold wind blows through the crotch of my hunting pants. Once again I've ripped them out on barbed wire, knowing I had to hurry to beat Jim: knowing there were birds coming up. And now I'll have to stitch the pants again. The nee-dle so hard to push through the canvas. Oh I could wear suspenders and hike my pants up, but with them when nature calls you do a fatal dance. With that much time away from the bird field, Jim will have gotten into another covey.

But lo, I find Jim sitting. Can it be that late? Is the morning gone? I hunker down beside him, sliding my back on the chalk white and pale turquoise trunk of a giant sycamore. Jim digs in his shirt and takes out two PayDay candy bars. I take the one offered me and lean back, squinting up through the brassy leaves of the great tree. Then I look at the PayDay wrapper and ask him, "Why do you like these bars so much?" And he tells me, "Because of you . . . you like them."

I try to remember whenever I told him that. But we've been hunting together a quarter century. How could I remember? But still, I can't remember having said that. Strange how things become real for no real reason. I look at the peanuts in the candy. Then I must acknowledge, the years have melted all the recollections together. Like, if I can remember the shells loaded with duck feathers and string, then why not a statement I must have made about PayDay candy bars?

I chew the bar and feel the wet earth seep through my pants. So I stand and take a gray stone with me, throwing the stone from the high bluff where we rest, seeing it and hearing it strike the stream far below. And the older Lab leaps from the bluff and tumbles down the steep bank, running now into the water, his head going down, his nose going under the water, making the water ripple the way a marlin's dorsal fin does, and up Rene comes with that stone. He runs back, picking his way up the steep incline. He hands me the stone and stands there, grinning. I stare at the stone. It is the one I threw.

"It's the stone I threw," I tell Jim in disbelief.

He shrugs.

I turn back to the dog, saying in awe, "You brought me the stone I threw."

Rene angles off to the side and flops to roll in the grass.

I turn the stone in my hand, amazed, but say no more to man nor dog who make so little of it. Then without display, I slide the stone into my right-hand shell pocket.

The truce of the sycamore is over. Once again it's every man for himself. I walk more slowly now, there is game in the coat and it has weight. Besides, the quail have gone off to take a snooze. Only the panhandlers will be out at noon. So it'll be a long walk with little game.

I look far away where the hills turn blue, where the sky looks lavender; where the distant diesel locomotives labor up the angle of the hill, towing the long string of freight cars. Then I stop and hush aloud, "Where's the caboose?"

Jim hears me and says back, "What?"

"The caboose. Where's the caboose on that train?"

Jim says, matter of fact, "They took 'em off."

And I watch the train without a caboose work up the long hill and over its crest and away. It goes like an incomplete sentence. No caboose at the end. No period. No nothing. And suddenly it hits me. Everything is changing.

I stare at Jim's back. At the dogs. The fields. I feel the birds heavy in my coat. It has never occurred to me before. Always it was me and Jim and the dogs and the birds, just outside Buffalo, Kansas. Always Jim knocked me sideways on the covey rise. Always the winter sun came up orange like a hot branding iron. But now I have a panic coming up in me.

It is changing. The train had no caboose. All trains have had cabooses for a hundred years. When Dad took me hunting, locomotives were coal burners. Now they are diesels and Dad's no more.

Something cold and frantic grabs at me. It lingers just out of reach. Nothing where I can just point it out and say, "There it is." Nothing I can reach out and grab like I did that rock Rene fetched. But it is there.

I shudder and glance at the dogs to see if they've noticed. By now Jim is far ahead. I see the labored drive of his stooped shoulders, the bow of his neck. Then that thing that's hovered at a distance eases this thought to me. The thought acknowledges, "Jim is the best hunter I've ever known." I wait for more to form. Then it is there, for some reality wants me to know for the first time. The reality says, "There is a greater hunter . . . and his name is Time."

I say the word through dry lips, "Time." And I shake this thing off and gulp, then hurry to catch Jim. Hearing no more the hollow drone of the far-away diesels, sensing no more the unspoken voice that stopped me in my tracks.

Coming breathlessly up on Jim, I ram him. For the first time in my life I slam him with my shoulder and knock him forward, stumbling. And I yell, banging him still more and laughing, "I've always liked Pay-Days."

He turns to me, astonished, and curses, "What the hell?"

And when the next covey of quail comes up, I hit Jim on the shoulder so hard I think I jammed my wrist.

11

THE MECHANICAL DOG

The following article appeared in the April 1983 issue of Field
& Stream *magazine. One year later the author was asked to
judge the first hunting retriever test-hunt ever held in America.
At last, points were awarded to retrievers that hunt to the gun and
the dogs were tested afield on their hunting ability.*

I was invited "over there" to attend the International Sheep Dog trials and I was sitting with my English sheepherder friend, Ray McPher-
son. Ray won the world sheep dog championship the two times it was
held.

He says to me, "At these trials you see a lot of mechanical dogs. But a good working dog must oft times disobey his handler and work the sheep as he sees it must be done. And the shepherd—who may be a half-mile away—just can't see what needs to be done. At these trials, it's like moving dogs on a chessboard."

Then Ray stood and said, "Well, I got to go get my dog ready to run." He jerked a thumb toward the contestant working the mechanical dog and said, "What good would that dog do you over a hill? You know, if he had to work on his own?"

Ray put his finger on a very grave American dog development: the mechanical dog. Seen mostly in retriever trials, the mechanical dog is also evident in pointing and flushing circles.

And what is the mechanical dog? That's the dog the trainer has conditioned to do particular tasks because of rigid and sometimes preposterous demands by judges.

I first alerted the nation to this problem in these pages in the early 1970s. Since then, other dog writers have climbed on the kennel wagon and pronounced the need to do something about it. Great! Dogdom needs the help.

Here's what I mean.

Any retriever worth his rations will launch to water to fetch a duck. But in a field trial that's not enough. The duck may be placed in water so the dog is enticed to run the bank and then leap out for the retrieve. "Aha!" exclaim the judges. "That dog ran the bank." And down go demerits in the judges' books.

But the dog that scores well launches to water directly before his handler (and the judges), then turns sideways and swims parallel to the shore to get the duck. What a farce. The judges say it shows control, that it also shows the dog is bold for striking the water. "It shows," they say, "the dog is not timid in going to sea."

But in a real duck-hunting situation (which field trials are required to duplicate) taking all that time to retrieve the duck could result in 1) the duck, being a strong cripple, could swim away and dive beyond retrieve; 2) incoming flights of ducks could spook from the retriever swimming the shoreline (some duck hunters think this is the case); and 3) during the time it took the dog to get the nearby bird, any far birds—also shot down—might float away.

Now this is important. Field trials are required to simulate a day's hunt afield. That's what their charter says they must do. Yet, in the example we've just seen, good common hunting sense is thrown aside so judges can make differences in dog performance that don't make any difference.

There are several reasons for this, but first let me recall a conversation I had years ago with Talbot Radcliffe, premier English springer spaniel breeder in Anglesey, Wales. We were out training dogs and Talbot observed:

"We must always remember field-trialing is a game. It relates not to the field. It relates only to manmade trials.

"To win the game, you must play the game; you must know the rules, and you must accept the sport of the game.

"It is not a hunt. It is a game.

"In this country, we have fox hunting. And in fox hunting, we have point-to-point. Now point-to-point is to test the horse running cross country from point-to-point. All this done, of course, in the fastest possible time.

"Now, that is a test for a hunter. But from this we have developed steeplechasing over manmade fences on a manmade course with proper jockeys.

"Now this horse—this steeplechase horse—you never take hunting. Oh no! He is a specialized animal for specialized competition in a specialized game.

"Now, you come back to field trials for springer spaniels. You have a specialized sport, a specialized game, a specialized object. And to be successful in it *you don't have to go hunting*."

My eternal thanks to Talbot for taking the plug out of his gun on this one: no one could have said it better. And so we accept Talbot's view of reality. But there's a catch.

If field-trial dogs are not tested for hunting abilities in hunting situations, then that means they are not trained to be hunters, either. They're trained to pass nonhunting tests. Which further means that specialized animals win, and they're the ones chosen for breeding. Which means today's pups are out of field-trial winning, but nonhunting, stock. And then the naive guy or gal buys one of these pups to go hunting!

What does the hunter really need? He needs a dog that can hunt from dawn to dusk. Has the field trial tested for this kind of endurance? The hunter may need a retriever that can work all day in cold water. Is this trait tested at trial? The hunter may want a dog that will hunt from a car, boat, or blind. Are these characteristics tested at trial?

In other words, are dogs really tested to duplicate a day's hunt afield? The rules say they must be. But the fact is: they ain't.

Why's this? The answers are many. First, let's consider judging. In Europe, a judge judges and his decision is final. He is felt to be above reproach. Why, a judge over there is even permitted to judge his own son in a national. It's happened in England: George Meldrum was the senior judge when Bill Meldrum, his son, ran the Queen's dogs.

But over here? Judges are suspected, begrudged, doubted. Therefore, they have to make graphic, and drastic, differences in dog work so all contestants can easily see the error of the tested dog's ways.

For a judge to say, "I decree this dog's work to be best for he pleases me. He shows style and birdiness and desire and stamina and . . ." No way. It just won't be accepted.

That's why birds are dropped right before English springer spaniels at trial; and though the dogs are enticed to leap for the quivering, hot-blooded temptation—they can't.

Or, why the number of covey finds is counted at a pointer trial. No contestant can gripe at the judge for that. One dog found six coveys, the best any other dog could do was four. "So we have a winner!" Hardly. The four-covey dog may have run first thing in the morning when the birds were late getting out of bed. Or the six-covey dog may be suffering from progressive retinal atrophy and all his beget will have it. Never mind, can't you count? That dog won!

There's also the matter of variance. Retriever trials must be mechanical so each bird falls in the same spot for all dogs. How else can they be tested equally? Once again, the judges are not trusted. In England, one dog may get a strong, running cripple. Another dog's bird may fall before his nose. The first dog has a much better chance of scoring higher. Fine! That's the way it happens at field. That's hunting.

But over here that can't be permitted. No judge can be given latitude to judge. Rather, he must just compare.

And there's something else. There are way too many dogs running on the American circuit. Yet, only three days each week are traditionally set aside for trials. Consequently, every test is sudden death. Oh, the judges want to let all dogs finish the first series—that's the payback for the guy who drove 500 miles to attend the trial. But after that, it's put one foot down wrong and you're on your way home.

Which means the big dogs—the dogs that run constantly on the big circuit—must post faultless performance. And one way to accomplish such miracle work is to brutalize the dog into doing it. To kick and hit and shock and shoot the dog, for example, to keep him from running the bank to retrieve a nearby duck.

In my mail awhile back I slit an envelop and took a page in hand to have a lad exclaim, "Please help me. I've got to win."

I laid the letter down, rose from the typewriter, went to have a long draw of hot tea. GOT TO WIN!

That's what's killing the various species of gun dogs in America today. That's what's robbing them of their innate instincts to hunt and fetch. That's what's turning hard-driving, free-wheeling, self-thinking gun dogs into mechanical robots in fur coats.

I drank another cup of tea.

Finally, I returned to the typewriter and answered the boy. It matters not what I said.

When it matters is now. Now that I visit with each of you. You who are the gun dog trainers of America. Win! Win what? A ribbon. A trophy. A check.

What about companionship with the one true friend God gave to man? The love and devotion of a good dog. What about years spent in training, bringing the pup to dogdom, and the dog to season? To seasoned wisdom, where he thinks out each field situation. Where he watches the ducks above you, and you can read their flight in his eyes. Where one jump sideways tells you there's a rattlesnake in that bush. Where the cock of the ear, the set of the tail, tell you the quail are coming up.

Win!

I remember a president who said he had to win, and the result was Watergate.

As for me, I'd rather be right than president.

I win every time a dog of mine props his head on my knee and melts me with his soft eyes.

I win when the gimped-up old warrior that I have to carry across ditches finally goes on point and, trembling, looks back over his shoulder to say, "I told you I'd find 'em."

I win every time a coon dog can't be pulled off a den tree, a terrier goes into a badger hole, or a beagle gives voice in a distant glen. We now live in a world of manmade man. So, it's only natural such a man should have a manmade dog. Something he can move on a chessboard.

Something he can beat the spirit out of and render a remote pawn.

But I don't call that winning. I call that losing.

I also call that impudent. For in all this thinking is the assumption that man is smarter than the dog he's training. But the more we look at what man's doing to his dogs at trial, the more we realize this just ain't so.

Why, you know there are now field-trial people who never go hunting? Who never permit their dogs to go hunting? Do you know there are field-trial people who insist the handler never be called upon to fire a gun? Do you know there are field-trial people who don't have a dog in their house? He's away at the trainer's.

And someone writes me, or calls me, and first thing he says is, "You gotta know the breeding of this dog. Why, he's out of Field Trial Champion Watergate Foul-up." And I yawn. For I've been told nothing to indicate whether or not this dog will point or fetch. Oh, it may be the pup's sire was impervious to high-voltage, low-amperage shock, or he could take a ton of buckshot and not go lame, or he could stand up under a BB-loaded whip and not buckle. But what's that got to do with whether or not he's a gun dog prospect?

You see, most field trials now demand the dog deny his instincts. And to deny your instincts, you've got to be terrorized off them. The distant retriever is after the floating duck. He's not seen it fall, his trainer has told him it's out there. Out there somewhere. . . . And the dog is looking and swimming. And the handler is whistling and giving hand signals and yelling for the dog not to go to shore. But where's the duck? It's planted beyond the hourglass of land. That's right, the land pinches in on both sides to make a narrow channel. Any dog in his right mind is going to go ashore and run on land to hit water again.

But that's not the point. Retriever field-trial champions are not in their right minds. They're in the judges' minds and the handlers' minds.

And should the retriever touch land, he's out of the trial. He must go the distance by water. He must swim the channel.

So what follows during the next week? The trainer sets up the hourglass test again, and this time when the dog goes to shore he's beat off it, shot off it, shocked off it. If he ever stays off it, he may become a great champion.

Champion of what? What God-given dog instinct has been tested here? Does the dog in the wild have to avoid land to eat? Hardly. These are tests devised by men to please men. They have nothing to do with the nature of dogs. And they have nothing to do with hunting.

When you start to tamper with the nature of the dog—when you start twisting and reversing and denying natural instincts—you are essentially re-creating the animal. Re-creating him in your own image. Training up a dog not to be a natural hunter, but one that avoids man-made temptations in order to keep from being beaten to death. And the result is called Field Trial Champion?

Well, across this nation are men and women who aren't going to take it any longer. They're leaving the old established field trial circuits and coming up with more true-to-life, hunting dog tests.

It happened first with the pointer and setter breeds. People who no longer believe upland game has to be approached on horseback are activating foot-hunting clubs. People who feel pointers and setters are only half-tested by pointing (who also want the dog to bring deadfall to hand) are establishing the new shoot-to-kill trials.

Retrieverdom will be next.

And I don't mean the so-called gun dog trials put on as picnic events by field-trial clubs. We've had these for decades. I mean a completely new—*alternative*—system where retrievers must duplicate a day's hunt at trial. Where either the American Kennel Club establishes a separate gun dog testing system for retrievers or requires field-trial clubs to return to the covenants of their charters. Or, different parent organizations establish retriever-hunting trials.

In any event, new clubs (or old clubs with new emphasis) must be created across the nation with charters that *demand* they test hunting retrievers. The retrievers will qualify for a national testing, and we'll have co-champions. We'll have the present Field Trial Retriever Champions. And we'll have the new Hunting Retriever Champions.

The first thing we must do to correct a problem is to admit the problem exists. I've done that in many *Field & Stream* articles and one retriever book. Now I'm to the point Bob Crosby (the first three-time, all-around cowboy rodeo champion) used to talk about. "It ain't no sin to have lice," he'd say. "It's a sin to keep 'em."

We've all been party to driving gun-dogdom someplace we never intended. But no future sin can be permitted. The barbarism and in-humanity of training gun dogs to win on today's circuit—like lice—have got to go.

12

OL' DRUM

*In the early 1960s there were three zany waterfowlers who hunted
Cheyenne Bottoms next to Hoisington, Kansas. There was Doctor
Robert Moore, the vest-pocket-sized dynamo who was an All-Navy
boxing champion and ate roasting ears the way computer print-
ers throw a line on a page. With him was Jim Culbertson, who'd
moved to Hoisington to coach the high school football team, the
Cardinals. Doc was the team physician. And last was this
writer, whom the two of them permitted to tag along as ballast.*

*Probably the most novel lodging I ever had while hunting
ducks was that year I checked into Doc's hospital for a thorough
physical examination. My camo and waders hung from the room's
wardrobe rail. The nurses would awaken and feed me before
dawn, and up the curved drive, coming in his International Scout
(with a shotgun hole in the floorboard) and dragging a monstrous
airboat, would be Doc. Doc had all the gadgets. Even a duck-*

plucking machine in a small room from which he would emerge looking tarred and feathered.

In the evening I'd be released to join Jim, and the two of us would go to Doc's house for a duck dinner—cooked by Doc's wife Bea—and poetry. Doc loved heroic poetry; he had a lot of Charles Kuralt in him. It was the finest of all arrangements.

Well, Doc was a thoughtful sort, and he had Senator Vest's speech printed up about Ol' Drum, the hound, and gave everyone a framed copy. Mine hung over my typing table for thirty years. Then one day something prompted me to look up, push back, stand, and head for Missouri to write Ol' Drum's story.

Here it is.

Turn the clock back 122 years, bare your senses, and attend to this scene. The Civil War has been over four years. Nowhere has it left deeper scars and a more granite temperament than in western Missouri (they said, "Show me!") where two armies and assorted renegade irregulars had pillaged the countryside and terrified the people. Every Missourian knew of death and destruction, so his response had become quick to fight, to be self-sufficient, to forever hold a grudge, to be inflexible in his opinions, and demanding of justice.

Now, narrow your focus. It is rolling country, heavily treed, with intersecting streams that teem with varmints. We're five miles south of Kingsville, Johnson County, Missouri (some fifty miles southeast of Kansas City), down in the second bottom of Big Creek. Log cabins nestle in the clearings with packed-dirt yards, a corn crib, root cellar, and spring house. This night in October 1869, a faint kerosene lamp glows from the store-bought window of the two-room log cabin occupied by Charles Burden and his family. The members are busy washing dishes after supper or shucking corn to make lye hominy.

Charles Burden stands (he is a strikingly handsome, tall, thin man with an athlete's physique) and says he's going to check the stock before turning in. He walks out the front door where Ol' Drum, a five-year-old black-and-tan hound, rises from sleep on the front porch and ambles close behind. They walk in the sodden leaves of a wet autumn; frost will sugar the land white by morning. Suddenly, Ol' Drum casts to the left and heads down into Big Creek. Immediately he strikes game, and the yip of his find pierces the air. The race is on. And Charles Burden stands to listen to the mellow bawls of his prized hound as the dog puzzles trail.

Later, Burden sits in a rocker on his front stoop, smoking home-spun tobacco in his corn cob pipe. Suddenly, a gun shot claims the still night. Burden lurches forward, straining to listen. There is no other noise. But in his gut there's a wrenching hunch. He leaps to reach inside the doorway and grabs his hunting horn. He blows until all hounds appear at his feet but one—Ol' Drum. And somehow Burden knows. His brother-in-law, Leonidas "Lon" Hornsby, has killed his dog. For Hornsby has been losing sheep to wild dogs, and he has vowed he would kill the next one caught on his property.

Next morning Burden approaches Hornsby, who is pressing cider, and asks, "Lon, have you seen anything of Ol' Drum around here?" Lon replied he hadn't seen anything of him. Then came the question, "What about the dog you shot last night?" Hornsby said he hadn't shot any dog, but his hired hand, Dick, had. He added he thought the dog belonged to Davenport. Dick took Burden across the yard and showed him where he had shot the stray dog. Burden looked for traces of blood and found none. Then he returned to Hornsby and said, "I'll go hunt. It may not be my dog. If it ain't, it's all right. If it is, it's all wrong, and

I'll have satisfaction at the cost of my life."

On the morning of October 29, Ol' Drum was found just a few feet above the ford in the creek below Haymaker's mill. He was dead, lying on his left side, with his head in the water, and his feet toward the dam, his body filled with shot of different sizes. Burden concluded Ol' Drum had been carried or dragged to this place: there was blood on his underside, his hair was bent backwards, and there were sorrel hairs on his coat. Lon Hornsby owned a sorrel mule.

Burden headed for an attorney. Later he would tell another attorney (the case went to court four times), "When I found that Ol' Drum had been killed, I wanted to kill the man who did it. But I've seen too much of killings in the border warfare. And so I said, 'I'm going to go by law. I'm going to clear Ol' Drum's name. He was no sheep killer, and I'll prove to the world that Lon Hornsby killed him unrightfully if it's the last thing I do.'"

So came to pass the most noted dog trial in history on September 23, 1870. It concluded on a rainy night at the county courthouse in Warrensburg, Missouri, with the top legal talent of western Missouri arguing, what was by now, *the celebrated dog case*. One of the defendant's attorneys told the jury, "Such a lawsuit about a mere hound dog is of little value if not a neighborhood nuisance." But that didn't prove to be the case.

George Vest, principal attorney for Charles Burden, sat detached from the day-long proceedings. He was short, a bull of a man with thick neck, broad shoulders, fiery red hair, and a voice that would fire ice or melt steel as he would wish. All of Warrensburg turned out for the trial: it was like circus day. The restaurants were packed, the hitchracks taken, the livery stable filled. People who could not find accommodations intended to sleep in their rigs. And those who couldn't get into the courtroom peered in multiples through the courthouse windows, enduring a lightning storm and downpour. The sheriff had made sure no man entered the court with a gun. All inside sweltered in the high humidity. Only Vest never wiped his brow. As he was no part of these proceedings, neither was he part of the suffocation of the place.

For a moment let's examine the legal talent assembled for this hound's trial. Charles Burden had retained the partnership of Sedalia, Missouri's, John F. Phillips and George Graham Vest. The former would become a federal judge, the latter a United States Senator.

Lon Hornsby countered with Thomas T. Crittenden, who later became governor of Missouri, and Francis Marion Cockrell, who ended up in the United States Senate along with his adversary, George Vest. These were not mediocre men, nor had they met for a mediocre moment. Ol' Drum had pulled them all together for the most celebrated case in dogdom, as surely as he once rounded up every varmint that tried to take up residence on his beloved master's farm. And as these litigants made Ol' Drum immortal, the hound dog went a far way in making each of them a legend in his own time. None of them could eventually discount Ol' Drum's part in making their legal lives a success.

Now there was no court reporter for any of the four Ol' Drum trials. What is known about what happened there has come down to us from word of mouth. Men assembled later and reasoned together to put the court's testimony into writing. And this becomes important, as you will see.

George Vest stood. He rose scowling, mute, his eyes burning from under the slash of brow tangled as a grapevine. Then he stepped sideways, hooked his thumbs in his vest pockets, his gold watch fob hanging motionless. It was that heavy. And he said, "May it please the court," and began his oratory.

Gerald Carson, writing in *Natural History*, December 1969, relates: "Vest began to speak quietly and earnestly. He ignored the day's testimony. For about an hour he ranged through history, poetry, legend, and classical literature, calling attention to sagacious and faithful dogs whom men have loved, quoting from the Biblical account of the dogs who came to lick the sores of the beggar Lazarus; citing Bryon's line in *Don Juan*, ''Tis sweet to hear the honest watchdog's bark'; and the graphic description in John Lathrop Motley's *The Rise of the Dutch Republic*, of how a dog had prevented the capture of William of Orange by the cruel Duke of Alva.

"After pointing out the weaknesses in the arguments of opposing counsel and drawing attention to the law applicable to the case, Vest appeared ready to conclude. But then he moved closer to the jury box. He looked (someone remembered afterward) taller than his actual five feet six inches, and began in a quiet voice to deliver an extemporaneous oration. It was quite brief, less than four hundred words."

These are the immortal words Vest spoke:

"Gentlemen of the jury, the best friend a man has in the world may turn against him and become his worst enemy. His son or daughter that he has reared with loving care may prove ungrateful. Those who are nearest and dearest to us, those whom we trust with our happiness and our good name, may become traitors to their faith. The money that man has, he may lose. It flies away from him, perhaps when he needs it the most. A man's reputation may be sacrificed in a moment of ill-considered action. The people who are prone to fall on their knees to do us honor when success is with us may be the first to throw the stone of malice when failure settles its cloud upon our heads. The one absolutely unselfish friend that a man can have in this selfish world, the one that never deserts him and the one that never proves ungrateful or treacherous is his dog.

"Gentlemen of the jury, a man's dog stands by him in prosperity and in poverty, in health and in sickness. He will sleep on the cold ground, where the wintry winds blow and the snow drives fiercely, if only he may be near his master's side. He will kiss the hand that has no food to offer, he will lick the wounds and sores that come in encounters with the roughness of the world. He guards the sleep of his pauper master as if he were a prince. When all other friends desert he remains. When riches take wings and reputation falls to pieces, he is as constant in his love as the sun in its journey through the heavens. If fortune drives the master forth an outcast in the world, friendless and homeless, the faithful dog asks no higher privilege than that of accompanying him to guard against danger, to fight against his enemies, and when the last scene of all comes, and death takes the master in its embrace and his body is laid away in the cold ground, no matter if all other friends pursue their way, there by his graveside will the noble dog be found, his head between his paws, his eyes sad but open in alert watchfulness, faithful and true even to death."

The jury erupted in joint pathos and triumph. The record becomes sketchy here, but some say the plaintiff who was asking for $150 was awarded $500 by the jury. Little does that matter. The case was appealed to the Missouri Supreme Court, which refused to hear it.

What does matter is the eulogy to Ol' Drum has now been translated into most every language on earth and has been printed in excess of 200 million times.

Both litigants were bankrupted by the proceedings. They returned to their homes, living one mile apart, and time eventually healed their differences. At that place where Ol' Drum was found lying in the creek with the sorrel hairs embedded in his coat, a monument has been erected which once contained stones from every state in the union and practically every nation on earth. Before the new county courthouse in Warrensburg now stands a life-size bronze statue of Ol' Drum.

And if you journey five miles south of Kingsville, Johnson County, Missouri, tonight, you'll likely hear the plaintive call of some hound dog coursing the stream's woods, giving voice of his find, the night air ringing like an empty oil drum struck with a sledge at the music of his going.

There will always be an Ol' Drum. And a man to defend his honor.

13

The Lion Hunter

I *told you we can't get far, nor stay far, from Grand Junction, Tennessee: the crossroads of America's sporting dogs.*

You'll remember Herman Jenkins, the weatherman of Grand Junction. One afternoon Herman told me, "Paul Rainey was the richest of all the dog men whoever came around here. I knew him, everybody knew him. He was the black sheep of the family, you know, so they cut down his inheritance and only left him forty million." (And that was in the early 1900s when a hamburger cost a nickel.)

"While hunting in Alaska," Herman continued, "he lassoed a polar bear that was so big it drug his yacht part way up on the ice."

I told Herman, "Now that's hard to believe."

And Herman came back, "I know it. But Paul chloroformed that bear, loaded him on a flat-bed truck, hauled him through the streets of New York, and gave him to the Bronx Zoo. He named that bear the Silver King."

Well, that was enough for me. I stood up and headed for the door. As I did I yelled back over my shoulder, "I'll see you."

Here's what I found.

Life was never big enough for Paul Rainey (1877–1923). No challenge thrown could thin his sporting blood, no dare could match his contempt for danger. Nor was there a horse that could carry him fast enough, nor a beast that could charge ferociously enough. Life was that pale, that dull. So Paul colored it by racing sports cars, playing polo, riding to the steeplechase, yachting, womanizing, hunting, and on one occasion taking on and defeating Germany, single-handed, during World War I.

His family called him Poor Paul since his Cleveland-based, coal-and-coke-baron father cut off his inheritance at $40 million because of the son's "reckless ways." The no-nonsense, penny-pinching father wished Paul could be like his elder brother, Roy. Roy didn't squander money, nor did he risk his life romancing danger. While Paul was out racing automobiles, sensible Roy was content riding a bicycle. (That's actually how he got around.)

Paul entered gun dog history when he showed up at the National Bird Dog Championship at Grand Junction, Tennessee, about 1901. (He would have been twenty-four.) He watched the trial, liked the country, enjoyed the people, got to talking to them about quail and coon and fox hunting. Whereupon, he immediately decided this would be a great area for his base camp. Not a place to stay, mind you, but some place to regroup between safaris. Shopping about, he found the nearest place he could assemble 30,000 acres (he needed that much land for fox hunting) was some rolling country ten miles north of New Albany, Mississippi, near a place called Cotton Plant.

Visit there today, view the remnants of the Rainey suzerainty, and you'll find history and re-creation buff, Mrs. Shelby McLarty (her husband Hugh owns a furniture factory down the road) serving as hostess to Paul's memory, directing the inquirer to, "Not miss that dog food oven . . . it's down there to the left by the road . . . with the tree growing out of it."

"Mr. Rainey kept four-hundred dogs," Mrs. McLarty, who now owns the place, will tell you, "and he was very picky about what they ate and how they were housed. Each had its own kennel. And sometimes Mr. Rainey, himself, would cook the food. He would kill a steer a day to feed his pack."

Dogs on hand were Trigg hounds, English pointers and setters, airedales, German shepherds, English fox hounds, retrievers, beagles, and "bear dogs."

On the day I visited the wind was blowing cold enough to smart. Mrs. McLarty braced it out, directing me this way and that, saying, "Don't miss the polo horse barn . . . it's round and made of bricks. We just got it rebuilt.

"And this was Mr. Rainey's trophy room." She swings open the door. "At first it was a ballroom. He'd have trains go about the country and gather up young ladies to come dance with his fox hunting visitors. Oh, how this place must have glowed. He had two men whose only duty was to make sure all girls got back on the trains by midnight. They'd be escorted down the cedar-lined sidewalks, across the road, and into the private railroad cars parked at Mr. Rainey's siding.

"At some of Mr. Rainey's parties he would give each girl a fur stole for attending."

I look at the rugged, natural stone fireplace: high and mid-center poses an "R." It graces the polo stables, too. I have seen pictures of this room when it was said, "Not one inch of wall could be seen . . . there were that many trophies hanging there."

Mrs. McLarty tells me, "And don't forget to stop and look at those four blocks of concrete with the steel rings embedded in them. That's where Mr. Rainey kept his pet black bears. One of the bears was always at the door to the house, to greet the many visitors. And there were all sorts of animals he brought back live from his hunting trips. Deer would come up and eat out of your hand."

I walk on to the country-club lawn and brace to the cold wind. Leaves skitter past. It's easy to imagine the Fourth of July picnics Rainey hosted: he invited 5,000 people each year. If you lived in the county, or beyond, you could come. At Christmas, in the very ballroom I just left, a strange Santa (so very tall since Rainey stood 6 feet 4 inches and weighed 225 pounds) would give each employee's child (or children) a great sack with two handles to carry away the sweets and toys.

The same man, mind you, who brought the National Fox Hunting Championship to Mississippi, who found his lodge too small to house his guests so he built a Paris-style hotel in New Albany, and who loved soda pop so much he built his own bottling plant (and wanted the pop cold so he built his own ice company). When the cash couldn't come fast enough to handle all his expansions, he bought a bank in town, as well as an interest in banks all over the state.

So it was that Poor Paul, who never worked a day in his life, found his investments making more money than he inherited. With that kind of income, why not take a $500,000 hunt to the North Pole? He did. He shot walrus from kayaks, and got the elusive (at that time) musk ox. Then went after the giant polar bear that dragged his boat up on the ice before throwing off the lasso. Never mind, Rainey leaned over the boat's gunnel and slipped the infuriating rope back over the raging bear's neck. True story? Yes. Named Silver King, the polar bear lived out the remainder of his life at the Bronx Zoo.

Rainey continued to expand his Cotton Plant holdings. He bought a 23,000-acre duck preserve in Vermilion Parish, Louisiana, a racing stable in Long Island, and later, a large plantation known as Forest Glenn in Kenya, Africa. The Kenya purchase came about after Rainey sat in his trophy room and lamented to his friend (and chief dog trainer and huntsman) Er Shelley that there was no more sport left in America. Tennessee wild boars, Texas coyotes, Rocky Mountain grizzlies, and Mexican jaguars were too predictable, too obtainable. Nothing was tricky enough nor mean enough nor fast enough to give him a challenge. Whereupon, Er Shelley laughingly remarked, "Then Mr. Rainey, I guess you better put together a pack of lion dogs and go hunt Africa."

Rainey leaped from his chair in shout, "That's it. We'll do it."

The safari left soon after, and Rainey hunted lion and leopard with hounds and horses every day (except during the infrequent business trips to America) for six continuous years. The hounds were simply Mississippi coonhounds and a string of bear hounds bought from the legendary field-trial immortal Jim Avent. The horses were trained as polo ponies so they could spin in a flash to evade a lion's charge. Doing so, they could give the hunter a split second necessary to snatch his rifle from the boot and fire.

Some Africans hated Rainey for his "folly." But mostly, they hated him for proving them wrong. They said no pack of hounds could hold a lion. They said the terrain with it's claw brush and ant-bear holes would destroy the horses. They said not even a polo pony could dart sideways from a lion's charge.

But the ostrich farmers did not agree. At the turn of the century, lions were wiping out this main crop of Kenya. The farmers begged Rainey to rid them of the vermin. And he did—one time leading a party to shoot nine lions in less than thirty minutes. This brought the authorities down on him. Rainey had been the first sportsman ever to photograph African wildlife with a movie camera: the films revealed Kenya to the world as a hunter's mecca and Rainey to the authorities as too effective. However, the many safaris being booked made the Kenyans realize it could bring in more money than ostrich feathers.

The movie-making amused Rainey. He did it grudgingly. He'd much rather be break-neck riding. But he finally found hunters who would go with him and abide by instructions. The lions were to be prodded into charging the camera, but not shot more than thirty feet away. Thus their momentum when stone dead would slide them to the feet of the photographer. Most hunters said, "You're nuts." Finally, Rainey got a hunter named Harold Hill (of Roosevelt safari fame) to take the job. The man related, "I only asked that if I were killed, Rainey would provide for my widow."

The hunting party immediately found a young, male lion in some thorn bushes, and Hill tossed in some stones to make him charge. Just then, according to Hill, Rainey asked, "If your wife marries again, do I still have to support her?"

"No," he was told by Hill, "in that case, you're free of obligation."

"Good," said Rainey, "throw some more stones."

World War I broke out with no concern to Rainey. Yet, he eventually would go to various shipping/receiving posts and find his hunting supplies missing. "Why?" he demanded to know. "Because," he was told, "the Germans are blowing up the railroad tracks, and it takes a long time to get them repaired and move freight through."

Well, nobody was going to screw up Rainey's hunting. Even if he had gotten up before dawn for 2,000 days and killed lion beyond count. The hunt must go on. Rainey summoned Er Shelley and instructed him to return to the United States. There he was to buy four of the best bloodhounds he could find, and then hurry back. They'd use the hounds to trail and catch those damned Germans and put an end to this nonsense so a man could go about his hunting.

It only took about four trips with the bloodhounds before the guerrilla party was trailed, caught, and killed. It was admitted by Kenya authorities that Rainey's action turned Germany's interest away from Kenya for the remainder of the war.

Yet Rainey apparently got to thinking about the war raging outside his lion-killing grounds and went to see about it. Maybe, he thought, he could ride a horse into it and force a charge. Well, no army would take him; he was 4-F. Never mind. He bought four ambulances and gave them to the French Red Cross. He drove one himself and carried the wounded. One day, on an impulse, he wrote a check big enough to build a hospital in Great Britain.

Tiring of the ambulance, Rainey convinced the French he should be the government's official war photographer. He took his lion camera to war.

At war's end, the lion hunt recommenced. But while taking a rest in America, Shelley informed Rainey that the dog trainer's wife objected to his being away all the time. Rainey exploded at such betrayal. He fired Shelley in seething anger. No man can worship two gods, grumbled Rainey. How could Shelley imagine that he could be shared by both the hunter and his wife? It never would work. It sure never worked for him. He remained a bachelor to his death—but he did not remain without women.

Rainey soon announced he was going to India to hunt tiger with hounds. And so he departed. But en route he angered a mysterious fellow (yes, it was all about a young gal onboard ship) who told Rainey, "You shall be dead before sundown of your next birthday."

Rainey guffawed at such nonsense, telling the man, "That's preposterous . . . for you don't know that tomorrow is my birthday."

The following afternoon Rainey fell ill and died with his head in the lap of a doctor's wife who once came to Rainey's Cotton Plant estate for a party and never went home with her husband. All aboard the ocean liner remembered the strange man's threat. It seemed that Rainey was killed by voodoo, or something that mysteriously powerful.

"Bosh," surmised Er Shelley, the dog trainer. "Paul Rainey once hurt his head bad in a steeplechase fall. Thereafter, he could never drink. And drink he did, I understand, at the party where he insulted the man."

Whatever happened, Rainey was dead at forty-six. The world never saw anything quite like him before or after. Those who knew him well said he was totally fearless. Yet, this writer suggests that Rainey hunted for something in life that was harder to obtain than any grizzly or lion. The one thing he hunted hardest, he never could find. He died hunting for some meaning for life and for himself. In the end, then, the ultimate hunter never got his quarry. Put that in your lion gun and wait for thirty feet.

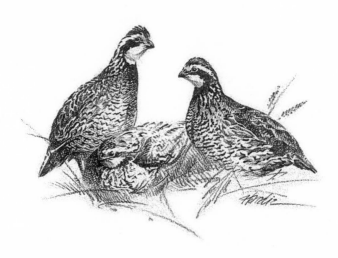

14

THE INNOVATOR

Rainey's immortality has as its base the almighty dollar. But for Er Shelley, his dog trainer, it turned out to be luck and wit.

Meet the most influential gun dog trainer who ever lived. The first man to package dog food, first to train with planted pigeons, and first to trigger a retriever's fetch by pressing a pinched nerve. He's also the mentor of a legion of gun dog trainers who went on to immortal fame.

Er Shelley (1874–1959) was the most brilliant, innovative, financially successful, adventurous, and luckiest gun dog trainer America ever produced. His feats are legion. But his one best trait was his captivating charm and bearing which enabled him to meet and earn the patronage of the gilded rich during the flapping twenties and the dust-bowl thirties. Of this we'll see.

Er was the first to train Mississippi Trigg hounds to hunt African lions—and hunted them practically every day for six years in the employ of the fabulously wealthy sportsman, Paul Rainey. More importantly, Shelley was the first to train bird dogs with planted pigeons; first to perfect the nerve hitch (with which he taught guaranteed forced retrieve) and the chain gang (with which he cured gun shyness); and was one of three trainers to ever win on the bench with a field-trial dog at Westminster Kennel Club. But he went the others one better. He took that bench dog and won the National Bird Dog Championship at the Ames plantation in the same month of the same year. That was Pioneer, national champion, 1906. Shelley was also the first dog trainer ever to make enough money to leave an estate when he died.

And that's strange considering his name: Er. We find it in Genesis: Chapter 38, Verse 7. "Er was the first son of Judah out of Shua," it is written. "He was slain by the Lord as a wicked man." Hardly prophetic. For if anyone ever found favor with the Lord, it was Er.

How else could he have bought a rustic mansion on one-hundred acres in today's downtown Columbus, Mississippi, and pay for it with two bird dogs? The house still stands atop a steep hill where his daughter, Virginia Dornan, and her husband, Don, greet us.

We walk beneath pine rafters, the wood as thick as an elephant's leg, toward the afternoon light; there's a sun room to the west, and this couple take their middays there watching hundreds of song birds come to the fifty pounds of seed scattered each week.

Virginia Dornan is strikingly attractive, poised, and disarmingly gracious. She seats me before a two-foot-high pile of newspaper clippings about her father. She talks as I leaf through the yellow-edged lot.

I hear her say, "My father became interested in hunting and hunting dogs while attending school in Edmore, Montcalm County, Michigan. His father was a hotel keeper on the stage coach route, and that building stands today. It's a registered historical landmark."

Virginia hands me a biography her father penned. "I began training dogs quite young," he writes. "It was back in the early '90s. I trained a setter in 1897. In 1898 he was better. So people came to hunt with me and my dog found 18 covies. They said that was the best they had ever seen and I should run him in the field trials. I had never heard of a field trial. He was entered at Lakeview, Michigan, in November of 1899. The dog placed second. And it was enough to cause me to become interested in the sport."

Flush with good fortune, Er Shelley headed south to bird country where from 1900 to 1907 (by his own testimony) he was the winningest trainer on the big circuit. Then fate threw him out of the saddle. It was just that simple, and that complex.

Here he was out training dogs, and he fell from his horse and broke a leg. And who should come down the lane but Paul Rainey the millionaire sportsman bachelor who Don Dornan says, "Got $3,500 a day from his inheritance, and that was before income tax." To which Virginia quickly explains, "And Paul Rainey was always broke. He had to borrow money from his sister."

Anyway, there's Er on the ground with a broken leg and a magnetic charm; Paul Rainey would have it no other way than to carry the dog trainer back to Cotton Plant and doctor him to his health.

Thereafter, until 1920, Er was dog trainer, general overseer, head huntsman, and "good ol' buddy" to Paul as they hunted the world. But it was not all easy. Er writes in his jumbled memoirs, "If Paul Rainey said the moon was green cheese, it was best if you countered, 'I've often observed that myself.'" The death-defying, reckless-riding, hard-living Rainey would accept no opposition, nor tolerate any disloyalty.

"My Mother," says Virginia, "was giving birth to me and there was

Dad way up in the Rocky Mountains with Rainey hunting something. Mom wired him and told him to come home. Dad had to cross the mountains in winter snow on a pack horse to get back to Mississippi. Mom told him, 'That's it. It's me or Rainey.' When Dad told Rainey his wife objected to the trips and he'd like to stay home and care for the plantation while Rainey hunted—the result was the sack! It was that final and that quick."

You think Er cared? In no time he was training for the public out of Columbus, Mississippi. Then he went with Detroit-based W. H. Hutchings' shooting preserve at Union Springs, Alabama. In the 1930s Er met H. L Pratt, who Virginia says was president of Standard Oil of New Jersey. He accepted the position of gun dog trainer, huntsman, and general host on the oilman's Goodhope Plantation at Richland, South Carolina.

Now get this: It's the Depression. Some of America is standing in soup lines; executives have been reduced to selling apples on street corners; my own father—who rebuilt automobile starters for a living—was making $56 a month. That's journeyman's wages for seventy-two hours a week. And how's Er doing? Well, his journal tells us, "The pay was generous but I more than doubled my salary by selling dogs to guests."

His salary: $500 a month, plus free housing for his family, a furnished car, a maid, all utilities paid—everything! And Er had written into his contract that he would supply Pratt with thirty-eight bird dogs for his hunting pleasure. But Er could also have an equal number to peddle to the gentry if they took a liking to any one performer.

Says Er in his memoirs, "One fellow, an Oklahoma oilman named Urshel, took a liking to one of my young pointers and asked the guide about it. When he heard the dog was mine he told me he'd like to have his private handler come over and give the pup a try. Of course I agreed. During our ride the man who handled Urshel's dogs kept up a constant chatter. Once he mentioned $5,000 and I decided that if the dog was worth $1,500 to a poor man like me, he would be worth at least $5,000 to Mr. Urshel. When I was asked the price I said, $5,000, and got the check right then."

Er had learned how to deal from Paul Rainey. He had sent Er back to England to gather more hounds for lion hunting, and on the return ocean-liner trip, Er met the second son of an established English greeting-card scion. The boy had been told to take a strikingly beautiful blonde girl, get her aboard ship, remove her from England, and be rid of her.

Virginia Dornan tells me, "My dad happened to mention he was going to Abyssinia [Ethiopia] to take motion pictures. And the girl said, 'I'd like to go with you.' Whereupon the second son said, 'That'll be fine.' So, when Mr. Rainey met them at the dock he immediately saw this blonde. Rainey was a lady's man, and he inquired about her. Daddy said she was going to Abyssinia. To which Mr. Rainey said, 'How much is this trip going to cost you on your own?' And Daddy said, 'About $5,000.' And Mr. Rainey said, 'Well, I'll tell you what I'll do. I'll give you the $5,000 for your trip, and you leave the girl here.' So the girl was left."

But don't think Er didn't earn his money with Rainey. On their very first lion hunt Paul Rainey let Er ride right into a lion sulking in a thicket. Rainey knew the lion was there; he just wanted to see what would happen.

And when Rainey showed up in New York with the polar bear he'd lassoed and named Silver King, it was Er who reckoned they could chloroform the beast and tote him right through town to the Bronx Zoo on a flat-bed truck. Er sat on the bear to detect movement and give a chloroform booster should it move.

Yes, Er Shelley was a man of many parts. And the above does not fill out his legacy. He wrote three books: two on bird dog training and one on hunting big game with dogs in Africa. He assigned himself bright young prospects and made gun dog trainers out of them. Clyde Morton, who won the National Championship eleven times (an all-time record) was one of his pupils. There's a picture of Er, Clyde, and two other men in the Dornan living room standing behind an absolute straight line of bear dogs, retrievers, and pointing dogs—eighty-eight in all. The way I see it, to do nothing more in life than get eighty-eight dogs to line up, sit, and stay would be worth entry into the Field Trial Hall of Fame.

Er was inducted into that august circle in 1957.

Virginia tells us, "He was eighty-five years old when he died, and his hair stayed black until he went to the hospital, then grayed all of a sudden. Daddy was always a slim man, never more than 140 pounds, something just under six feet. He was very well preserved and enjoyed telling people how old he was. But then he lived his entire life in the out-of-doors.

"He was a nature lover," she says, "and the one thing he hated most was a man who would shoot over his limit. Daddy was a leader in that. One of the first conservationists. And he meant it."

Well, Er I'd liked to have ridden the river with you. You were quite a man. Don't know when another like you is apt to come along. Yet, when are the times in which you operated ever to be seen again? You came to life when game was plentiful, restrictions were minimal, fields were virgin, and men were loose with their wallets. Even with a broken leg you could make a silk purse out of a sow's ear. Rest In Peace.

15

JOHN OLIN: A TRIBUTE

There was another dog man whom I dearly loved that deserves inclusion in the Pick of the Litter. He was John Olin, head of Winchester Arms. But most important to us, John just may have been dogdom's greatest benefactor.

John Olin was a gilt-edged vestige of the champagne age who lived into the light-beer era: he died two months shy of his ninetieth birthday.

A small man (what was he, five feet, four inches?), he was, nevertheless, nitro in a thimble. Plus, he was wit and charm and grace, as well as clout.

But above all, to me, he was my friend and the friend of dogs. He is gone now and I miss him, and the dogs will miss him, too.

So I pen this tribute by letting John have his own say (he'd like that), selecting bits and pieces from the talks we had together.

These nuggets of Olin say something behind the scenes about the man whose horse, Cannonade, won the 100th running of the Kentucky Derby and whose retriever, King Buck (at that time the only dog to ever appear on a U.S. stamp), won back-to-back National Championships in 1952–53—only to be matched by Saighton's Sizzler, Olin's English springer spaniel, who did the same thing in 1970–71 in the English springer nationals. (Incidentally, Sizzler was bred by Talbot Radcliffe, Anglesey, Wales, who tutored us in *The Mechanical Dog*. Remember?)

Sometimes these excerpts of our conversations may show an indifferent regard for man by this industrialist who chaired many of America's great corporations; but always, there is the helping hand extended to the animal. After all, it was Olin who had his engineers make an aluminum wagon tongue so the mules pulling his hunting wagon wouldn't have so great a load to carry.

So here's Olin by Olin:

John was a cherubic, pink-cheeked, twinkle-eyed man who could have played Santa at Macy's. But there was a rascal in him. He, Cotton Pershall, his retriever trainer, and others were hunting birds in Canada when—well, let John tell you:

"Messina is where we crossed the St. Lawrence to get where we were shooting. We were in a motel there; it was Sunday. We could shoot Sunday, but we ran out of whiskey. Even the game commissioner couldn't help us on that one. There just weren't any liquor sales in Canada on Sunday.

"We were puzzled as to what to do, so we came back to the motel. We were letting our dogs out to air when an American came up to me and said, 'I wonder if you can help me. We've bought some of this Canadian bourbon whiskey, Crown Royal. It's supposed to be awfully good. I'd just like to know if you can tell me how much of this we'll be allowed to take back through customs without having to pay duty on it. I don't know what the regulations are, and I thought maybe you could help me.'

"And I said, 'How many bottles you got?' And he said, 'I've got a half a dozen.'

"And I said, 'Well, I'm afraid you're in trouble. I'm quite sure the limit is one bottle. Beyond that, I think they'll confiscate it.' To make a long story short, Bill, I bought the extras . . . *but I've always been ashamed of it.*"

That was John. A force to reckon with when it came to creature comforts, but if dogs were involved . . .

"I'll have to admit I am the damn fool who started OFA (the Orthopedic Foundation for Animals)," John once told me. Then he explained: "I remember a dog that belonged to General L. J. Sverdrup from St. Louis. He was a very close friend of mine and quite a competitor in the amateur running of Labradors.

"Well, Jack Sverdrup gave the dog away. He wanted to give it to me, but I didn't want it. So he gave it to [name deleted by author] who was an avid field-trialer, and the dog ran on the circuit for a long time under a professional trainer. This trainer was always shooting the dog with hydrocortisone before he could run him.

"This trainer and I used to get into arguments. And that interested me. *What was that dog's real trouble?* I'd wonder. We did have some dogs around here with hip dysplasia, and that got me further steamed up on it. I just didn't think it was arthritis, and I didn't think you could control it by shooting hydrocortisone into the hip.

"That brought me into contact with Wayne Riser of the University of Pennsylvania veterinary college. We got to talking about the thing, and he had some ideas that this was hip dysplasia. Being of the curious type of mind that I am—I always wanted to get the answer to the question *why*—I kept asking, "Why do dogs have it?"

"Riser said the university would like to get into this thing and try to unravel it and so forth. I don't know if I made the first grant to them or not. But I did give them some money to look into it, and that was the creation of the Orthopedic Foundation for Animals. And the investment in hip dysplasia at the present time is in the neighborhood of between $800,000 and $1 million. [John fails to point out that this is his money alone.] We're never going to be able to eliminate hip dysplasia by any quick remedy. It's an inherited disease, and there is no way to eliminate it. But we're getting closer and closer to reducing it."

This was John the dog philanthropist. But there was John the Shrewd and the Blessed as well.

He delighted in telling this story: "King Buck came up for sale. I could have gotten him for $5,000 [today, that price would be $50,000], but Paul Bakewell, III queered the deal. [Bakewell was a St. Louis, Missouri, insurance executive who won the *Field & Stream* challenge cup seven times. The cup signified the national retriever championship of the year.] He bid him up. But I had to have the dog. So, I ended up paying $6,000 for him. A terrible sum in those days. Why, you could buy a house for that.

"But, King Buck qualified to run in the national a year later. They had a Calcutta going, and I had a friend bid him in for me at $350. Well, King Buck won the thing and won the Calcutta as well—a sum of $7,500. So you see, I had just won the National Championship with a free dog, and they even gave me $1,500 for doing it."

So it's true: those who have, get. But in John's case, they also give . . . and he gave. Only once did he ever tell me this story:

"Back in the '40s I had a wonderful racket down in the south. In those days, I went and shot for a week with Walter Edge down at Sunny

Hill Plantation. Then I moved over and shot a week with Walter Teagle at Norias. Then I came up and shot a week with Bob Woodruff, just twenty-five miles southwest of Albany, Georgia. That's three weeks of quail shooting the best plantations in this area.

"But when I was at Bob Woodruff's—I forget what year it was—he lost half of his dogs. And they didn't know what killed them. They just died in about three or four days.

"Bob Woodruff had a deal with Walter Teagle, the latter was in the field-trial game, and any dogs not of field-trial caliber would go to Woodruff for his shooting string.

"While I was there, half of Woodruff's dogs and half of Teagle's field-trial dogs died. And no veterinarian in that part of the country could put his finger on it.

"Well, I graduated from Cornell, so I got Jim Baker of the veterinary school down here for a week. And when he was finished, he identified it as distemper. He went back to Cornell, and Teagle and Woodruff and Olin [notice how Olin again refuses to use the designation, "I"] financed the beginning of the veterinary virus laboratory at Cornell.

"And that, Bill, was the beginning of the cure for distemper in this country."

John Olin was champagne in crystal, but I was branch water in a tin cup. I was born to that and reared to that and stayed to that. So, you can imagine the thanks I have for this man when you think of all the strays I had that either scratched themselves to death from the mange, got hit by cars, or dropped dead with distemper during the 1930s and 1940s. Distemper is a horrible disease: symptoms include convulsive seizure, vomiting, high temperature, diarrhea, coughing, pacing, optic-nerve damage, and pussy eyes. John, as far as I'm concerned, is due any good turn life presented him for his part in obliterating this humaneless killer.

But where John Olin could give a fortune to save some dog misery, he could turn right around and be misery itself to anyone dealing with him. Consider the case of the four milk cows.

John tells us, "My friends were after me to get a plantation in the south, especially around Thomasville, Georgia. But I didn't want to locate there. Too much night life and socializing. I had that up in St. Louis. That's what I wanted to escape. Plus, I wanted to go bird hunting.

"Well, I looked over four states and just couldn't find anything suitable. When I looked at the place that finally became Nilo [Olin's name backwards] during the 1940s, I didn't want it. Too many low spots that caught and held the rain—plus the place had been turned over to cattle, and the quail were few and far between.

"Well, we had a lot of on-again, off-again dickering . . . the owners of this plantation and me . . . and the first time we tried to get together everything was called off.

"Then a realtor contacted me in my New York office and told me the place was on the market again—same price. And I told him, 'All right, that's fine. I'll take it, but I don't want anything to do with the cattle he's running there. He'll have to dispose of them some other way.'

"And that all worked out, but later I realized the man had four milk cows, a separator, and a pasteurizing setup—everything you need for fresh milk and butter, and Mrs. Olin and I like that. So I told the realtor to tell the seller that the four cows had to stay. I told him, 'Cows aren't cattle.'

"Well, the seller said no. The realtor told me that and this is what I replied, 'You tell that damned Yankee that my family came from Vermont, and he only came from Massachusetts. Vermont Yankees are a damned sight tougher than those Massachusetts Yankees. The milk cows come in or we don't buy it.'

"Now mind you, here's four milk cows that can queer a 10,000-acre purchase, and the seller asked the realtor, 'Is that Olin so damned mean that he means it?' And the realtor told him, 'He means every word of it. If he doesn't get those four cows, he'll kick the deal right back in your face.'

"So," says John, chuckling, "that's how we got the property and the cows."

Tough and irascible, John Olin could be severe on a man, but he'd go out of his way for a dog. Consider: John Olin ended up at the Riceland Hotel in Stuttgart, Arkansas, immediately after King Buck won the National Championship at Weldon Springs, Missouri. John was going to take the national champ duck hunting.

Through the lobby both man and dog came. The man was heralding the dog's accomplishments and his nobility—setting up the drinks and cheering all to pay homage to this great champion.

And the National Championship trophy (a large silver bowl) was filled with champagne and lowered to the floor: King Buck will now have a victory drink. But the great Lab rejected the bubbly, so the champagne was poured out and water substituted. The dog lapped, the water was poured out, and once again champagne was poured into the bowl. But when one man was presented the bowl he refused to drink, saying, "I'll not drink from a bowl after some dog."

And John Olin leveled his gun-metal eyes on the culprit and in terse finality ordered, "You get this S.O.B. out of here before I throw him out."

The man was escorted off the premises. The dog stayed. And now they're both gone: dog and master. Both champions. I hope they're together this very day on a pond that never ices up, in mud that never pulls your waders loose, in a blind that never lets the iced mace of winter's wind blow through. And I hope nothing but big fat mallards fill the sky and toll to the call and fall to the gun right before the blind.

For John and King Buck would like that, and they earned that. Happy Hunting, John Olin. You'll be missed.

16

JOHN BAILEY: A GOOD SHOOTER

John Olin and I had a mutual friend. He was John Bailey, of Coffeeville, Mississippi, who was not a millionaire, but he lived like one.

This came about when two northern mercantile brothers sent an agent south looking for a place to hunt quail. The agent stopped at Coffeeville, and the local Nestors told him if he wanted to find quail he should first find the young John Bailey.

Later, when the brothers went on to other pursuits, they gave the land to Bailey. And in this pine and lespedeza paradise John Provine Bailey possibly became the greatest bobwhite hunter the world has ever known.

Early each spring, John Provine Bailey would fill his pockets with lespedeza seed and walk his northern Mississippi field. He would thumb out each seed, one by one, from his gnarled hand, and where each seed fell it would be struck into the earth by his boot heel.

But walking and planting 4 miles of lespedeza a day wasn't seventy-five-year-old John Bailey's purpose. Rather it was to harvest the bobwhite that would eat the seed. Bobwhite is what John raised for harvest.

And during sixty-two years of recorded hunting, John did harvest with his shotgun more than 18,000 bobwhite quail.

I'm not sure the world ever saw the likes of this before; and I'm pretty sure it won't see it ever again—especially since John maintained a bona fide lifetime shooting average of 66 percent, cataracts and all.

Nor was it just bobwhite John took to heart and table. He also hunted dove, ducks, geese, turkey, Hungarian partridge, prairie chicken, and squirrel. As a boy with slingshot, he'd sneak from his bedroom window at night—his mother, whom he called Nundear, forbid this—and run south of town to hunt with his mentor and friend, the old, black man named Granathan Hayes. They'd chase the 'coon and 'possum, and clean, skewer, and char-grill their catch over an open fire with a bounty of sweet potatoes laid in the coals. They knew they were numbered among God's chosen.

You needn't have hunted with John Bailey to know him. Just go to his birthplace—and burial place—Coffeeville. His heirs come back there to tend John's beloved 2,000 acres of Quail Hills: they dote on him and keep all the faiths. John's neighbors and townsmen glow with warmth and pride when they tell tales on him—good tales. The local and national press put the ink on John. For example, *Field & Stream* covered him three times. Twice by this writer in October 1977 and August 1981, and once by Nash Buckingham in December 1943.

But the best way to know John is to read his hunting record. It's been here at my house for days now, through the courtesy of John's immediate heirs—his twin daughters, Jean Bailey Kirk and Joan Bailey Bowen.

It's the largest loose-leaf cardboard folder I've ever seen, bought in those pre-computer days of hand-written business ledgers. It weighs eight pounds on my bathroom scales and is filled with touch relics as well as written fact.

Things are Scotch-taped at their ears against the hard covers, the tape running with amber ooze after these long years. There's a duck feather here, a turkey stamp there, a hunting license stuck to a page. And through the record is a detailed sixty-two-year account of the hunt: the names of dogs and horses and men; the guns and shot loads and hits and misses; and the weather and cover.

But the treasure to me are John's word-keepsakes. Things written by Theodore Roosevelt, Zane Gray, Ralph Waldo Emerson, and Hambone. The words aren't always quoted; some have no authority listed. Instead, they just pose there, and I hunch some of them are John's. I like to think so. Especially when I read:

"The smell of Christmas in a country house, the bugling of hounds running a fox on a moonlit night, a boy whistling to keep the boogers away as he drives the cows home at dusk, the sound of waves wasting away on a lonely beach, the gaiety of a fish fry or squirrel stew on a river bank under giant pinoaks, the smell of marsh before daylight with whisper of duck wings overhead, the look of a tired dog as you share a fire."

There's no note of man's great squeeze plays in John's hunting record, no mention of the heroes of our time. Nor any concern with the arena of man, abortion, commercial zoning, or automated bank tellers.

There are just the faint animal calls of a calm night recalled, the warmth of a stick fire, the rustle of leaves, the promise of the sun, the smacking of a dog's jowls, the whir of a bobwhite's scat.

The hunting record is John Bailey, ever alive, tucked away outside Coffeeville, with good hunts, good times, good books, and good fortune.

On the first page of that record is the true basis of John's life, plus a prologue to his death. For here he has scribbled, in lines that run up to the right:

". . . and one day the grasshopper will fiddle his last tune."

"Art is man's nature: Nature is God's art."

"The years you done spent is either the best help you've got . . . or else it's the worst handicap," attributed to Hambone.

"The height of folly is to live poor so you can die rich."

We'll devote lots of time to John's hunting journal, but first let's listen to his kinfolk talk of John's passing.

After I journey to Quail Hills lodge after John's death in search of still more source material on the man, his two daughters host me with a gathering of clan and friends. Jean Bailey Kirk recounts what she has written earlier in a Yalobusha County compilation of notable citizens: "John Provine Bailey, our father, was born June 2, 1907, in Coffeeville. A year later he had a baby brother named Joseph Foster.

"Now John and Foster were close, but they had different interests and talents. Foster loved things mechanical, but John dreamed only of the woods and green valleys and red hills around his home.

"He found a friend—an idol, actually—in the old Negro, Granathan Hayes, and they'd roam the countryside together. It was then his parents realized they could no longer hold their son back from his great love of the outdoors. They gave him a gun when he was twelve years old as a reward for making a seventy-six in Latin. It was a Sears and Roebuck $4.85 special. With that, John was released to his lifelong obsession, and devotion, of hunting birds . . . and he started his hunting record.

"He grew to be tall—6 feet, 1 inch—with the black hair and brown eyes of his mother, Pearl Provine Bailey. He was broad shouldered, but his hips and legs were so long and slim you'd wonder how they could possibly hold him up to walk the great distances he demanded of them as a hunter. Why he'd walk sixteen miles a day."

"And once," offers Hilliard Griffin, who sits in the circle of chairs at the lodge, a forty-year hunting companion of John's, "he ran home holding to the back of a horse and buggy. It was ten miles to town in the mud and rain."

I smile at this recollection. Jean continues, "Daddy attended Baylor Military Academy in Chattanooga and Mississippi A & M College. But he left school, and for several years lived in Greenwood—that's fifty miles from here—to learn the cotton business with his uncle, Brax Provine. This proved to be the ideal avocation for him, even though his father was in the mercantile business and offered John a legacy, the cotton business kept him busy only through the fall harvest season. The rest of the year he was free to hunt and fish."

Then Joan Bailey Bowen reveals, "For rainy days, he bought a local billiard parlor. He said little of this, but it is known he had a personal cue stick he would take to Memphis to hustle the dandies. Also, he had small bowling parlors scattered around, and he would slip into town without fanfare and post a bet on bowling with the locals. In later years he still enjoyed pool, plus dominoes. He told Jean and I more than once that his special cue stick helped put us girls through college."

Jean takes up the biography, saying, "Soon after returning to Coffeeville from Greenwood, he went to a dance at Water Valley, twelve miles north of here. Across the dance floor the grace and beauty of one girl caught his eye. She was Catherine Elanor Guinn. Daddy couldn't dance, but somehow he won her attention, and eventually her love. They were married October 23, 1928, at the Water Valley Presbyterian church. And he brought her home to Coffeeville to share his life and his dreams.

"My sister and I grew up to love the hunting life that was our heritage. And we did become tomboys, spending much of our time," she laughs, "trying to kiss our elbows, for we had been told that would surely turn us into one.

"We often hunted with Daddy and competed mightily to outdo the other—all to the joy of Daddy, but to the dismay of our mother, who was a lady of culture and art and home.

"In 1934, twin brothers from Detroit, Jerry and Tom Webber, came to Mississippi looking for good hunting acreage. They were merchants with money, and they struck up a deal with Daddy to buy them this place. He was their guide. And they came every year for over twenty years to hunt quail. When they became too old to hunt they gave the place to him. In 1969, John and Catherine designed and built Quail Hills [a huge log cabin]. They gleaned materials from the land: cedars for the walls and furniture, stones for the exterior and fireplace, and the hearthstones from a place where as a boy John used to sit and rest during the hunt.

"In their fiftieth year of marriage, Mother was suddenly stricken with a heart attack and passed away. Daddy buried her behind the lodge. Then five years later, Daddy died the same way. He'd been fishing for crappie on an April day. He had brought his fish home, cleaned them, and was going to cook them for his meal. But he died. And he was buried beside mother. Out there, you'll see it now, is the headstone he designed for the two of them. On mother's stone he wrote, 'A Great Lady.' And on his, 'A Good Shooter.'"

Joan Bailey Bowen offers, "Daddy buried those he loved out there. His horses, his dogs, his wife. On one horse's headstone he had engraved, 'A Good Black Horse.' On the grave of a dog, he had written, 'A Good Pointer Dog.' It was because of Jean's daughter, Kathy, that he chose the epithet on his stone. She was only three years old then, standing before that very fireplace when Daddy came in with a great many quail. She was very impressed and she said to him, 'Granddad, you sure are a good shooter.'

"So, that's what he chose to be remembered by through eternity. But his friends have objected, and out in the woods on this place they've erected a sign which says, 'A Great Shooter'."

The Miss America pageant comes on TV and the girls want to watch it, so I rise and walk out on the porch. In the dark I pull a chair up to John Covington, a successful soybean farmer who married one of John's cousins. I ask him about John Bailey. Covington is disarmingly bright. He'd be a Red Man scholar in Duck Head overalls, except he dresses like gentry and came to dinner driving a new Mercedes. He tells me, "Twenty years ago John Bailey gave my wife and me a wedding party. And he showed us his hunting record. I guess I didn't show proper appreciation because he told me, 'If someone would pay me $50,000 for this diary only to throw it in the fire I wouldn't sell it to him.' I knew right then that John Bailey needed a keeper.

"But you know, as the years went by and I learned more of John Bailey, I know he meant what he said that night. I'll tell you, he convinced me later when he said, 'Rockefeller makes money and I hunt. It's important to both of us.'

"John Bailey enjoyed what he did, and he did what he wanted to. No one was more successful in doing that than he was."

Francis Franklin, a retired highway patrolman who also married one of John's cousins, will tell me later, "I was driving by Quail Hills one day with a fellow officer and I told him, 'That's John Bailey's hunting lodge.' And he asked me, 'Is he a millionaire?' And I told him, 'No, but you can't tell the difference.'"

In town there's an 18x18-foot shack across the street from the cotton gin. It's a ramshackle shanty that's falling down, no corner is true, there's a sag in every board. Grass enters between the wall and foundation and runners cross the floor. Beside the door is a sign. It says, "Coffeeville Cotton Exchange." This was John Bailey's office: his empire. He paid the city of Coffeeville $55 rent a year on the place, and that was all he wanted to invest in doing business.

He'd told me years before when I was visiting him, "I had to find a way to make a living that wouldn't interfere with my hunting. I thought on it. Then I chose becoming a cotton broker. I did it for the same reason men become baseball umpires. Two hours work a day, six months a year. Only I've got it better than umpires. Nobody's throwing bottles."

Sue Arrington, John's secretary, writing in the weekly *Coffeeville Courier*, April 28, 1983, says, "John didn't care about money. He worked hard once to take care of his family, his girls, but after they were gone his needs were minimal. And the idea of accumulating wealth for wealth's sake was repulsive to him."

Russell Bailey, another cousin to John, tells me, "John Olin, the wealthy outdoorsman who owned Nilo Plantation outside Albany, Georgia, offered John Bailey a substantial sum of money to move down there and build up the quail population the way he'd done at Quail Hills. But John refused. Making a dollar wasn't his interest. And no way would he leave his beloved Quail Hills."

Now I must make this point. With such dedication to the hunting of birds, you, the reader, will do both John Bailey and this writer a great disservice if you assume John was a game hog—a shooter of the hungry bullet. To the contrary, John told me, "I impose limitations upon myself over and above those placed on me by the department of wildlife conservation. On some days, I'll only try for singles. On other days, I'll only shoot birds flying left to right. Limiting one's shooting can be made into a game. But above all, good conscience is the same as good sportsmanship."

Understanding this, I can now tell you John harvested 18,000 quail, but counting all birds he brought to hand, as I have done by adding up each entry in his eight-pound hunting journal, he harvested 32,803 authenticated birds in his lifetime: 30,000 of them within a few miles of Coffeeville.

But John put back far more birds than he ever harvested. He was years ahead of his time. He was the first to burn and the first to scientifically plant food and cover. The state of Mississippi named him Wildlife Conservationist of the Year on December 9, 1981.

And hoping nobody would ever add up the birds in his hunting record, he told me, "Everybody is too impressed with the number of birds they kill. I'd rather take eight or ten shells to kill four or five birds, and walk eight or ten miles to do it. The places that dog takes me is the reason I'm still out there."

So this was John Bailey, possibly the greatest, single treasure of bird hunting skill and knowledge America will ever see. In everything he did he was a force. Imagine, the United States Forestry Service threatened to put him in jail in 1941 because he wanted to burn his land. John lived to prove that's exactly what had to be done. He was right in all things birdy.

Attending the Coffeeville United Methodist Church where John Bailey taught the men's adult Bible class for twenty years, I asked his peers what John's favorite Bible verse was. I was told, "He loved Micah 6:8, but he loved Ecclesiastes 7:1 as well." Paraphrased, the verse tells us, "A good name is better than great riches."

Now, let's get to the Hunting Record.

John Bailey placed his life in trust with nature. It was an irrevocable trust, which he drew on till the day he died. To be sure he was a bird hunter and conservationist: this was his motivation. But he was also an athlete with superb coordination and microchip-quick reflexes: this was his skill.

Bailey maintained a lifetime 66 percent shooting average. His actual harvest for sixty-two years included 506 mixed-bag birds taken during eight trips to Canada, 9,788 dove, 4,417 waterfowl, and 18,037 bobwhite quail. That's for a total of 32,802 birds.

John Covington, who we met on the front porch, has told me, "John Bailey worked a heck of a lot harder raising birds than most folks ever do making money."

Hilliard Griffin, retired Coffeeville postmaster and forty-year hunting companion of John Bailey, reveals, "John liked to handicap himself in the field. He'd set up a sequence of duck species he'd shoot any one day. For example, the first bird had to be a mallard drake, followed by a green-wing teal, and so on. If they didn't come in that way he wouldn't shoot. Or he'd only shoot quail flying in one direction. Or he'd only shoot dove that came at drastic angles. And if a species wasn't doing well, he'd not shoot. One time when the ducks were down, he wouldn't go to Canada."

This writer shot birds with John, trained bird dogs with him, rode the countryside, and admired what he loved. I also was his patsy in many games of pool. Bailey could shoot this game with surgical skill, take on all comers bowling, and when he was young, draw $5 a Saturday afternoon (this was a week's wages then) from the members of an all-Negro baseball team in Coffeeville to insure them a win over the visiting team. His legend as a marathon walker on his quail hunts will be told for decades in northern Mississippi. When he was young an average hunt would be sixteen miles.

Plus, John was intense. He would not compete with a fellow shooter, but he competed fiercely with himself. If he missed too many quail he knew he should have hit, he'd wrap his gun barrel around a tree. One time he was shooting paper shells that swelled up in his pockets during a rain. A hunter that followed said he picked up enough discarded shells to last him through the remainder of the hunting season. The point is, when John went bird hunting everything had to work right—including himself, his equipment, his guns, his dogs, and later, his hunting horse.

But laying all this aside, the most interesting aspect of John Bailey was his hunting record. There he logged every hunt, every shot, every hit and miss. Not in flowing stories. But in a headline, or a box score, with skeleton-thin detail.

As John told me in 1977, "I'll meet men after forty years, and they'll say, 'Remember that day we killed thirty-four quail?' And I'll say, it wasn't thirty-four, it was twenty-two.' Somehow the gamebag gets heavier in memory. But the hunting record always lightens the load."

So, accurate recall was one purpose for the record. But more than that, each entry brought back a memory to John: the face of a hunting companion, the style of a dog, the savvy of a horse, the swing of a gun. And it brought back, too, his life: his youth, his prime, his senior years, and the world he hunted during all those distinctly different seasons.

John passed away just shy of seventy-six in April 1983. In a letter he wrote to me, dated July 1, 1981, he reveals, "Although I am only seventy-four, I have hunted in eight decades, from the teens through the '80s.

"I go through my hunting record and find something unique about each of those eras. Like when I started, it was horse and buggy gettin' there, no game laws, no land posted. I was learning the game, trained my first dogs.

"Then in the '20s I hit my stride, had unlimited endurance, big bags, my best dogs, got more capable at finding birds, developed as a shooter.

"The '30s came and I found myself no longer concerned with big bags. I began appreciating the game more.

"Then in the '40s I hunted somewhat shorter hours, got the first notions of habitat improvement, did more horseback hunting.

"The '50s saw dove shooting get popular, and we had low duck limits. More land was posted. And extremely dry and hot summer days caused poor quail years in 1952, 53, and 54.

"In the '60s I built Quail Hills and moved in. Deer hunting got popular in these parts. But quail habitat went down statewide due to new farm crops. But where habitat was maintained, or improved, the quail were still good. And yes, I had a great dog in Fin.

"It became mostly afternoon hunts in the '70s with ducks and doves hunted often. When I killed my quail limit Saturday, Feb. 2, 1974, it was fifty years to the day from my shooting my first limit. Not many men have had that privilege.

"In the '80s I've hunted 139 times from September 1980, to March 1981, with my going for quail, dove, and ducks all about the same."

The reason John wrote this letter was two-fold. First, note the date, July. Hunting season was closed: John was bored. Second, John always wanted to write for *Field & Stream*. He had two friends who did, Nash Buckingham and myself. He was asking me to help get him published. I say to John now, "Congratulations pardner, your copy's in. You made it!"

Now to the details in the record.

John starts by noting, "First quail I ever killed was in front [across road] from Uncle Rob. N. Provine's home in Calhoun county. It was a rooster sitting in a tree. I shot it with a .22 rifle in the summer of 1920.

"First one flying was bagged about ½ mile northeast of the Branum home, 1 mile north of Coffeeville. It was with Robert Gray. His dog Munk pointed the covey. My gun was a .12 ga. single barrel, 32 inch. It was Feb. 24, 1922.

"The next year I got a 12 ga. field-grade Ithaca double. Uncle Brax gave me a pointer pup named Belle.

"I got my first limit Feb. 2, 1924. I was with Leon Brower. Dogs were Belle and his dog, Fred. The place was 16th section of Eggleston place on Point hill." [Note: rocks that were hearth rocks at a house on this hill are now hearth rocks at Quail Hills.]

And so Bailey's life—which was his hunts—is started, day by gun by bird by place. Page after page. Over sixty-two years. And here and there are sprinkled summaries. Like "Most straight quail kills, 30, 17 one afternoon, 13 next a.m. Most straight one day, 22. Most birds killed standing in one place, 12. Did this 3 times. Most coveys found one day, 30. Most coveys seen in air at one time, 4. Most birds bagged in 1 day, 60, by 2 p.m., Dec. 12th, 1929, on Dog Creek, Calhoun county."

Within the daily log are tucked rare insights into John's rural Mississippi. He loved such stories and told them often. Other than hunting, I think storytelling was his greatest amusement. He tells us, under the title *Whisky Spring*, "In the mid-1940s man named [deleted] lived on our farm. He was helping me train a couple of hunting horses. I would give him money to buy corn for the horses. The horses continued to lose weight so I got 'smart?' and gave the man corn instead of money. But he got smarter, he made whisky out of the corn at this spring."

Apart from his record, John posted signs on his place to recall important happenings. Like "Nash Buckinghan's Last Quail." My favorite of them all, and there are many, is "$20 Hill." John writes, "In 1926 I was living in Greenwood, Mississippi, working in Uncle Brax Provine's cotton office. I bet a man $20 I would kill 30 birds on a Sunday. Leon Brower met me in Granada Saturday night and I took Bill [a dog] out to spend the night with me in a deserted cabin on Granathan Hayes' place." [The reason for all this stealth is John's mother didn't want him hunting on Sunday.]

John continues, "It poured rain. Leon could not get there the next morning so I had no hunting hat or coat. I couldn't wear my good clothes so I wore my dress shirt and pajama bottoms and started hunting. It poured rain until 2 o'clock and I only had seven birds. But when the rain quit I found a covey soon after. And out of that covey I got 11 birds with 10 shots . . . and knew I was going to collect that $20." He did.

Another sign on John's place reads, "REX'S FIRST POINT." John tells us in his record, "I took Rex out to try in Nov. 1956. Price $50. He pointed his first covey here. I rushed back to Marshal Langham to pay him. Rex was 1½ years old and untrained. I took him to a trainer named Milliard Crawford who offered me $500 for him."

Another note in the record tells us, "On July 21, 1926 [John would have been 19] I ran off to Scuna river: took rifle, cooking kit, bread, salt, condensed milk, cocoa, and potted ham. Didn't have a blanket but slept very peacefully by a camp fire with the coals, wild cats, and mosquitoes. Killed one squirrel and had three cups of cocoa every meal. Also bread and meat. Piled up a big pile of wood in fire before I went to sleep but it burned up about three o'clock and I woke up with one leg in hot ashes."

In a summary of 1954–55, John relates, "Mac [his bird dog] went down a lot. Lost his hearing and except for a few days his nose was way under its former power. He trails, and birds in the woods flush most of the time before a trailing dog. Buck was better. He started hunting singles and dead the last two weeks and did nice work on the woods' coveys. Molly is timid, loves to hunt, good nose, but too cautious. False points too much and is afraid to go to bird when she smells them. This is three straight bad years of quail hunting. I don't seem to have patience with my dogs or my shooting when I miss." John was forty-seven when he wrote this.

John never considered himself a dog trainer, but he was a rare observer. He once told me, "The average dog will run through woods and point birds over general areas. But the superior dog learns something from the first covey in the woods. If the dog has sense, or instinct, he will hunt the same strata throughout a patch of woods once he finds the elevation of the first covey. If the dog finds the first covey feeding on acorns and other mast 30 yards from the ridge of a hill, then the dog can reason that other coveys will be feeding on similar food in similar cover at a similar elevation."

John's record continues, "We hunted the hard places (Thursday, Feb. 8, 1960, cool, dark). Dr. Leonard mountain area. I got 4 straight singles in the thick pines out of the Simon Thompson covey." [With John every thing was named, even the coveys.] "Saw Fin [his dog] running down a hill, smell a bird. He could not stop so he leaped at least 12 feet over the bird, tried to turn in the air, and landed pointing the bird. I called Hilliard [Griffin] and he killed it."

Bailey and Griffin hunted ducks often, John being successful enough over the years to collect thrity-four migratory waterfowl bands that were dated from January 27, 1940 to December 13, 1980.

Griffin tells us, "John was very competitive, but he was very thoughtful. He gave his game away, especially to the old people in town. John competed with himself. He'd have made a good golfer, for he was always trying to beat percentages he'd established. He would shoot against par."

The record goes on: "Favorite gun, 16 ga. double Ithaca. Most deadly gun, 16 ga. Rem. auto. Best percentage gun, 12 Marlin pump.

"Best shots I ever saw, Nash Buckingham, Memphis writer; Orson Munn, New York lawyer; and Bob Avent, Greenwood cotton man.

"Most birds killed on rise in one day, 47. Killed 261 birds in 8 straight hunts. On all days hunted in 1934, average 18 coveys a day. Most birds killed at one shot, 4, did this 8 times. Most quail killed in one hour, 32, did this twice. Killed 15 quail on 3 consecutive covey rises and 13 out of the 4th covey rise making 28 birds. Those birds was taken with 29 shots in about 50 minutes.

"Bagged 128 birds on 9 straight covey rises with double gun. Hunted 27 days straight on 2 occasions. Most birds with one box of shells, 26, taken Jan. 22 and 23, 1959. Most birds killed out of 1 covey, 20. Did this twice. Highest shooting percentage any year 78 percent in 1929."

Then midst all this data, John reasons, "This is the day which the Lord hath made. Rejoice and be glad on in it." Or he'll quote a friend, like Jerry Webber, who said, "If we never missed it wouldn't be fun to hit."

Then there'll be a thought from Zane Grey and another from Bob Brister, *Field & Stream*'s Shooting Editor. It says, "And the old snow goose had survived another first day on the marsh."

I would have more chance at stuffing all the shot John fired after birds into one shell casing as to try to put this man's life in one article. The richness never ends, like, "About 1954 I was training 2 pups, a pointer, Bo, and a setter. Both pointed their first singles at the same time. I didn't want to show favoritism by going to one pup as they were about 40 yards apart and if I went to one pup I knew the other pup would run his bird up when I shot. So I stood halfway between them, say 20 yards from each dog, and when one pup flushed his bird I killed it and then turned and killed the other." I'd say that was mighty thoughtful, and very skilled, bird dog training.

As interesting as such revelations are, I just may love the simple and revealing disclosures best. Consider this: "March 31, 1922. Stayed out of school and hunted. April 7, I killed a lark, Robert got a squirrel. April 23, I got a Hans Wagner baseball bat. April 27, I found a dove nest with V. D. Nelson. May 15, shot sling shots."

We have much to thank John Bailey for. He lived the ultimate bird hunter's life and left us much to treasure. And in this regard I beseech each of you to start a similar record for yourself.

We take our hunts home in taxidermy mounts, bronzes, prints, and all manner of touch-and-sight relics. But you'll find nothing has the value and meaning of recording your day-by-day outings afield. Hit or miss, each entry is you. And the result will become a joyous journal for yourself, your heirs, and perhaps, for generations of readers for decades to come.

John Provine Bailey's tombstone says he was, "A Good Shooter." That's how he wanted to be remembered. And I grant you, that's what he was. But for me, and more important for all of us, he was a superb chronicler of a hunting age the world will never see again.

Scattered through John's record is the simple declarative, "And one day the grasshopper will fiddle his last tune." John seemed obsessed with this thought. But I can tell him now, "John, you were one grasshopper whose tune will never end."

17

SOMEWHERE NEAR OLYMPUS

So far we've sampled the world of gunners making great gun dogs. How about the world of gun dogs making a great gunner?

The name of the town rhymes with "swim," not "begin." That's how the natives say, "Sequim." Sequim is a retirement village sandwiched between the Olympic National Park and the Strait of Juan de Fuca, some sixty-five miles west of Seattle, Washington. It's a place where old men go to do all those things they've worked all their lives to be able to afford to do.

But often they've waited too long to stalk the deer, dig that clam, toll that duck, net that salmon. So, Sequim is sometimes called Widow Village.

Except for its scanty rains, which means the sun shines most of the time (and is duly commemorated by place names such as Sundell, Sunny Brook, and Sunny Meadows), Sequim's never been famous for anything. Anything, except Dave Barnes.

Though the title is contested by *Guiness Book of World Records*, Sequimites say Dave's the world-champion clam gulper. As Bill Sullivan tells it—an amber-eyed, kinky-haired giant who keeps you thinking you've seen him playing the banjo on *Hee Haw*—"Once each year, in the world competition, Dave bellies up to a table, removes his false teeth, readies his elbows, and eats about four-hundred clams in eight minutes.

"Dave doesn't eat or chew the clams. He doesn't even swallow them—you don't see his Adam's apple go up and down. He just packs his mouth full, keeps it full, and pushes a continuous jam of clams down his throat."

"The way he does it," Bill rests the mass of himself on the counter of his Discovery Bay Grocery Store & Café (a store that features a walk-in cooler built of logs) and adds, "usually the guys on each side of Dave puke. That don't bother Dave none, so he just wins. When he's finished, he drinks a quart of orange juice and a pint of vodka. Then he eats a steak and has a few beers. Old Dave's the champ."

While listening to this story, I've read the underside of a cap off a bottle of Ranier beer: "Rocknest, Wash., Annual giant condor fly-in and yearly search for missing personnel of ranger station #8."

What next will I be asked to believe? That's why I'm here in Sequim, to learn as fact what I've been told to believe.

I walk to the door of the grocery and look out at the bottle-green water of Discovery Bay. I try to figure where Bill's put his crab pots when the man tells me, "Chuck Dryke's place is just on the other side of Sequim. Five miles maybe. You can't miss it." He pauses to add, "You say you're going there to see his kid shoot?"

I nod, "Yes."

"Well, shoot he can," the man's voice booms in affirmation.

Chuck Dryke's gun dog kennels, trap and skeet shoot, duck walk, and high tower are a testimonial to a man's doggedness. He built it all by hand over a twenty-year span. Every drop of concrete hand mixed and poured by the bucket; cedar shake shingles hand-split in the back yard; pond dug out of a peat bog with a junked piece of road equipment floating on jury-rigged logs.

Chuck meets me at the door, sticks out a rough-barked hand. It's all split' dirt-packed fingernails, scabs and calluses spotting the skin like the butt of an Appaloosa horse. I've not met the man since I walked up to him at the National English Springer Trial and praised him for shooting pheasants—never saw him miss—at eighty yards out. He thanked me, but added, "If you want to see some shooting, you ought to see my boy."

I'm here to do just that. But where's the boy? The place is a scout camp or YMCA: there are boys everywhere. I'd learned in Sequim that Chuck's a surrogate father, the Pied Piper of the Olympic Peninsula. As one woman put it, "Chuck's a den father. More than that. He gets kids out of problems their parents wouldn't even tackle. Teenagers bring their problems to Chuck when they're too explosive to take home. He's really a friend in need."

Chuck and I walk toward the gunning range. The man has little to say. He's already told me, "God gave man two ears and one mouth, so I think he wanted us to listen twice as much as we talk."

At the range there's a cattail of a lad—6 feet tall, probably 130 pounds. He's shooting a .22 pump, hefting the chamber after each shot to throw the spent shell high in the air, shooting the flying casing so it screams in ricochet. He misses on the eighth shot. Chuck asks, "Matt? Do you have time to come here?"

A response is not automatic. The question calls for thought. Finally, Matt ambles toward us, head down, a mop of brown hair in his eyes. The boy looks up, his eyes are the blue of Mennen pre-shave with flecks of gold about the pupil. He says, inaudibly, "Hello."

"That was amazing gunning," I encourage, nodding out to the place where he'd had his stand.

Matt doesn't acknowledge my enthusiasm; he continues to look at the ground.

Chuck says in peppy voice, "Matt? Would you like to go through our old routine?"

Matt shrugs his shoulders in embarrassment.

While they're getting set up, I pry out of Chuck—these two guys run out of conversation immediately following "Hello"—the fact that Matt started shooting at the age of six. He shoots 1,500 .22 cartridges and 350 12-gauge shotgun shells a week. He's only had the money to enter one tournament—the Al Levin Memorial Shoot at Bremerton, Washington, an open trap shoot held in a high wind that saw many shooters refuse to toe the line. He won. Matt shot a 95 from the 21-yard handicap.

The longest string of hits for Matt occurred when he was thirteen—he hasn't tried since—when he shot 280 mixed skeet and trap before missing at trap (Station Five).

Upon learning this, I asked, "Well Matt, what'd you say when you missed?"

In shy reserve, the boy stands mute. Chuck takes over, explaining, "Arnold Riegger, who'd shot 1,341 straight trap, was here that night. Arnold's from Longview, Washington, and works for Boeing. Well, when Matt missed, he looked at Arnold and said, 'I've got a thousand more to go. Out of sight, really, but I'll keep trying.'"

They're all set up now, and the show begins. Chuck announces, "Matt does the good shooting and I just clown around." The man slides clay pigeons down the barrel of a Browning over-and-under and shoots them before they hit the ground. He puts two clay pigeons on the gun stock, flips them, and dusts them. He puts a clay pigeon on each foot, leaps to send them sailing, and hits them as they go.

I ask, "Chuck, on a regular trap and skeet and doubles and tower shooting, how often do you miss?"

"About once every two weeks," he tells me.

Now the boy is ready. He's on a unicycle. He rides around the skeet range with a shotgun and shoots everything his dad pulls. Matt positions himself at Station Three, skeet. He rides toward Station Eight. A clay bird comes from one house or the other in rapid order. He gets them all—from the hip.

Yes, from the hip. As a six-year-old, Matt couldn't get a shotgun stock to his shoulder. So, the gun was squeezed between his arm and body to let the kick dispense in air. Later, Chuck wrapped a rag around the gun barrel—now the stock's in Matt's shoulder—so he couldn't sight. Consequently, he never looks at a barrel—shotgun or .22. With both eyes open he focuses only on the target.

Starting at Station One, Matt walks the skeet range, shooting from the hip. He turns in a twenty-four.

I ask Chuck, who dreams of the day the boy makes our Olympic team, " What will the Olympic coach say if he sees Matt shooting like that?"

"He won't believe it. I doubt if he'll be able to say anything for a while."

Matt rests the shotgun against the clubhouse and picks up a borrowed .22; his was stolen the previous week. But any gun will do. Matt doesn't check for elevation or windage on sights. He never looks at them. Chuck walks across the gunning range with two balloons filled with water. They're going to stage a trick. But, Matt jumps the gun. He shoots the balloons out of his dad's hands—spraying him with water. Chuck turns in chuckle, exclaiming, "So you want to play, huh?" Whereupon he blows up a balloon and just leaves it in his mouth. Matt blows it away.

Now, Chuck stands beside Matt, throwing quarters in the air. The boy pings them to oblivion. Next, it's pennies. Then, it's dimes. Chuck switches targets—some 2-inch aluminum disks, 1/2-inch thick. The disks are thrown into the air, where Matt tries to keep them riding. He runs his string to three hits on one aerial target.

Fishing in his pocket for shotgun shells, Chuck asks, "You ever see anyone shoot the shot out of a shell?"

Is there need for an answer? "Hell no, I've never seen anyone shoot the shot out of a shotgun shell. But, then, I've never seen a lot of things I've seen today."

The shotgun shell is thrown in the air so it rotates end over end. Matt shoots the shot out of the shell. He does it again, and again, and again. Then Chuck grabs a shotgun and shoots the shot out of a shell. He says, "You got to know where the edge of your pattern is."

I'm standing dumbfounded, my hands full of shotgun shells with their ends blown off. Never once was the primer or powder touched.

The show goes on—shades of Buffalo Bill and Annie Oakley. Matt shoots six hand-thrown clay pigeons with a pump gun before they hit the ground. Now he switches to a .22 and hits four. Later, he throws clay pigeons between his legs (like a center in football), picks a shotgun from a picnic table, and gets two clays. Now Matt has his dad throw while he shoots the first rock, tosses the gun to his dad, picks up a second gun, and dusts the second rock before it touches ground.

The two of them move toward the trap house. Matt shoots heads of cabbages so they explode, potatoes, eggs, charcoal briquettes . . . Chuck says, "We run out of ideas and things to shoot!"

"Well, how about game?" I muse.

"That's what you're having for dinner tonight," I'm told. "Matt shot a deer running across the flat out there."

I sit in the shade of the clubhouse and admit, "I've never seen anything like it. The boy is good. But the boy's got problems. How will he ever break out of here without a dime? He can't afford to go to shoots. No one knows he exists. He's Olympic material. And here he lives at the foot of America's Mount Olympus. It's ironic. So close, yet so far. The State of Washington ought to get up a kitty for Matt. He'd be a favorite son that could take them far. As we say, a good son of a gun."

Chuck interrupts my contemplations, saying, "We'll show you more later. Let's eat." As I'm rising I look out at Matt. He's just thrown two clay pigeons, flipped a shotgun behind him—like pool players who heist a cheek on the table where there's a lot of green between them and the cue ball—and hits two birds from behind.

I stand to watch a few moments more. Matt has picked up a .22 and is popping clay pigeons. Only, he's shooting fragments. He hits the clay pigeon; takes the largest fragment and gets it; switches to another fragment, gets it, too. All in all, he makes four hits on one target.

I'm shaking my head as we walk toward the Dryke house. That's where Mrs. Dryke died last year, ending a long illness. I look back at Matt and intuitively know more things than I've been told. It's dark and the boy's still shooting. How do we say it? Shooting in the dark?

Chuck is talking, this man with the gentle wave in his hair, the light blue eyes, the soft voice—a gun dog trainer and shooting instructor. "Here at Sunnydell we have a different philosophy on gunning. It's not like the old days. You can't learn on game. You've got to learn to shoot at a range. But the mission is not to seek and destroy. A limit of game is not our goal, but a good day in the field. So, along with gun schooling we motivate good sportsmanship and try to get the kids to really appreciate the out-of-doors.

"The most important aspect in shooting is the connection between the ground and the gun—and that's the gunner. It's a matter of concentration. You must have a good positive approach. You can't just wishfully think you're going to hit that target, because there's a lot more sky out there than there is birds."

Chuck stops in step and conversation. He surveys his forty acres where hardly anyone ever comes, for Sunnydell's sixty-five miles and a ferry boat ride from the people; and when they do come over, the many recreational opportunities of the peninsula provide stiff competition. Now the man says in that voice of one who must issue information during the silent part of an opera, "This is the way man was meant to live."

He moves on now, his pace picking up, his voice raising, "In shooting," he explains, "primary focus point is the target. Never look at your gun. The gun needs no sights. Get both eyes open. Secondary focus point is the barrel. And the target and the barrel are related only when they come together. The biggest fault with most shotgun shooters is their eyes are on the barrel and not on the target. It makes the swing too sluggish. You've got to burn a hole right into the target. If you're looking at your barrel, you've got to refocus from 2 feet to 40 yards. There's no way this can be done consistently."

I stop to survey the trout pond where Chuck's ducks fly in for gunners who shoot this preserve. Chuck describes these clients as "men who find the hills get steeper, the mornings come sooner, the birds fly faster, the rains get wetter. They come here at noon and get a good shoot."

I smile in acknowledgment. We'll all be there. Then I ask, "If getting your eyes off the gun is the most needed advice for young gunners, what's second?"

"Flinching," he says. "Flinching! But a man can keep from flinching through mental discipline. The best way is to have someone else load your gun behind you. You don't know if he put in shells or not. You may have empty chambers. You'll call for a bird, sight, squeeze, and just get a *click*. Soon, your reactions will be the same for a loaded gun as they are for one that's empty."

I laugh at the simplicity.

Chuck adds, "No doubt the biggest fault of misses for old timers is a flinch. It's caused by the noise, the recoil, and the results of previous shots. If you've become insecure, you know, you choke up, you stab at it, you jerk it, you flinch. So, confidence is what one must build. Shoot it as though it's yours. And shoot it as though you had an empty gun."

Chuck and I sit down to the venison feed. I see Matt tug on an orange-and-yellow reflective motorcycle helmet, throw his leg over a bike, and wheel away as he *varooms* from the premises. Gun dogs bark down at the kennel. Ducks quack.

Finally, the dust and noise settles.

Later, there's no venison on the serving plate, and the steamed butter clams lie a tumble of empty half shells.

And Chuck talks. Who said he wasn't loquacious? I can't shut him up. He's telling me, hours later, as my eyelids droop, "There are basic steps to gunning, just like a dog has heel, sit, stay, and come and a horse has whoa, giddyup, back, and turn. Shooting is stance, swing, lead, and follow through. There's hardly any way you can jump right in the middle of it."

My head jerks up. I mumble, "That's it."

"What?" asks Chuck.

"In the middle of it . . . I want to jump right in the middle of bed."

The man smiles and nods, then says, "Good night."

I head for my room, but pause in the dark of the hallway to realize, somewhere there is a fifteen-year-old-boy riding his bike in the moonlight on the foothills of Mount Olympus. And back home his dad sits alone at a dining room table, praying that one day the boy will climb another mountain by the very same name.

I do so hope it turns out that way, for a mountain's no mountain at all beneath the feet of a stepper.

"Step high," I hush in breath to Matt, then find my bed and sleep.

When this article appeared, the people came—just like in the movie Field of Dreams. *At the 1984 summer Olympics in Los Angeles, Matt became the first American ever to win an Olympic gold medal in skeet.*

18

The Best Year Yet

I wrote what follows on New Years, 1986. But what I say fits you, fits me, fits any year. It's seldom any of us grasp a truth. I tried to come close on this one.

It's five minutes until midnight, December 31, 1985.

My wife, Dee, and I walk into the chilly darkness behind the house—the dogs scattered about us—and we raise our toast of diet pop, hear the *click* of glass, and wish each other a Happy New Year. Someone down in the village sets off a string of firecrackers, and the dogs run to the road, barking. We must laugh at their intolerance. Nothing must enter their world, not even sound. We all go inside for bed. It's 1986.

But I send Dee on ahead and linger at the kitchen table, seeing a reflection in the glass of the back door. It is quiet. The wall clock ticks down the hall; there is the drip of the kitchen faucet, the sigh of wind brushes through the piñon beside the house. Two dogs stay behind with me, and I must adjust my feet and chair to get between them. I prop my head in cupped hands, rest my elbows on the table top, and wonder: What do you do with a used year?

You don't stuff it like a trophy and hang it on the wall. Nor do you recycle it like an aluminum can. Oh, you can regret a year, that's for sure, when you get the W-2 form that comes as a penalty for having lived one, for having worked one.

But it's funny, you know? You can't do one thing with a used year, and yet *you put every minute of yourself into it.*

I stand and walk out to the back porch. The stars are bright, a coyote yodels in the canyon. I peer into the darkness. A thought forms. I've had it before. It comes now and then as each year comes and goes. It says something like, "The years we live only seem to make a difference. They really don't. What really makes a difference are life forces. Forces that seem to come to each of us at birth. Forces that determine our nature. That never leave us. No matter how hard we fight them, they always have their way."

Let me explain with a man and a boy.

I wasn't there. It happened so fast I couldn't be there. Admiral R. R. "Doc" Lyons lies lifeless in a downstairs bed at the old ranch house on Maui. Before the heart attack in 1983, Doc slept upstairs. But now his wife, Ba, has coaxed him to this lower room, so there will be no stairs to climb. And besides, this is the sunniest of all rooms. The morning light comes first here; it patterns on the floor and walls and turns the white-and-yellow wallpaper to fresh-separated cream. Out beyond the windows are plumeria and eucalyptus trees; their leaves sparkle in the morning light. Beyond is the old horse pasture, tall now with crowded grass.

Doc lies motionless, as though a great volcano has finally come to rest. He has just been released from a short stay in the local hospital. I remember once telling Ba, "Doc reminds me of the top dog in the kennel, walking stiff-legged and throwing exasperated threats at all who come near for fear they'll pet him and he'll have the humiliation of their watching him melt." For Doc is really easy to love, and he wants to love back. But for the idle passer-by, Doc is hard to understand.

I sensed this the first time we met. It was the force. The same relentless force that drove Doc in the dog field also took a sixteen-year-old enlisted seaman (he lied to the recruiter, saying he was seventeen) to retirement thirty-one years later as a two-star admiral. And for that matter, that same force had to be at work when Doc wooed and won the most eligible belle on the Hawaiian islands. For Ba was beautiful, bright, and bold. She was also a Baldwin: one of the Big Five Hawaiian families. It was the Baldwins who sold the island of Lanai to the Dole pineapple people. It was the Baldwins who gave Haleakala crater to the American people as a national park.

In the room of light the curtains are drawn. The room is cool and gray now, and Doc does not move. Nor does he speak. What could he be thinking, if he's thinking at all? Of eighty-three years of living? Of the years at sea? The day the kamikaze hit his ship? Or could his thoughts go back long before that? Hunting rabbits near Gardiner, New York, on the small family farm, the fifth of six boys? Or after he retired from the Navy, the business deals, the board membership of all the Boy Scouts on the West Coast?

Yet, what is this? A great bounding moves closer in the tall grass. It is white and black and shag of hair. Its tongue lolls, the heave of its sides is apparent. It's an English setter, knocking a hole in the Maui skyline. Doc's mounted on a buckskin mare he calls Kerosene. They progress in a great lope, a whistle lanyard dancing crazily on the man's chest, the black Acme Thunderer whistle perched in his lips. He is a force in form, thick of chest and shoulder and thigh, but his hands hold the reins gently, the man sits the saddle lightly. His voice sings out over the tipped land, "Hooo boy...hoooo." For Hawaii is one of the few places on earth you can run dogs above the clouds. The land reaches that high, and it must consequently be tipped that much (like children's mountains: inverted ice cream cones).

Oh, how we all looked for this dog for Doc. He had told me before, "This may be my last dog." And he must have told others. For we swept the mainland to find Doc a dog that could win. A dog that could take the six-month quarantine and come out without missing a stride. It was a tall order to fill, but such a dog was found and shipped to Doc, even though his health would not permit him to train it all that much. So others pitched in, especially Doc's young dog apprentice, Michael Abreu. And the two of them groomed the dog, Kapalaea Marching Drum, and pointed him to greatness by preparing him for the running of the Hawaiian Open Championship.

But during the running of the Lanai trial, word is received by Mike Lyons, Doc's oldest son, that the admiral is failing. At that same time, the dog, Drum, is lost on the field. If not found in time, he must forfeit the brace he runs. Mike, as scout, dips in and out of the gullies on horseback, over the knolls, around the brush. He has given up and rides to the judges to report the dog is missing. But the dog has come hurtling back on course, making a fine find, then running to front, a great white-and-black streak of bird-hunting determination.

Now Mike is standing in the small Lanai airport. He must get home to Maui. That call was urgent. When the light plane is seen in the distance, both Michael Abreu, Drum's handler, and Joe Cooke, a relative of Ba, arrive at the airport to tell Mike that Drum has won. With only six weeks training between quarantine and the running of the Hawaiian Open Championship, the dog has become a champion.

The three men climb into the light plane, Mike holding the great trophy.

It is in the wan light of evening, on the creaking wood floor, that Mike approaches his dad. The man lies motionless, propped up on pillows. The son tells him, "Dad, Drum won." Then, in an expression Doc always loved to use in those times of hard-won victory, Mike says, "We wiped their eye, Dad."

Doc's right hand raises slowly from the sheets, and the hand curls over the lip of the koa-wood and silver-bedecked bowl. His eyes show no acknowledgment. But the hand grips the wood rim. The son stands for a minute, then backs away. Joe Cooke and Michael Abreu enter the room and try to say something. They leave Doc clutching the bowl. Two hours later, Mike takes the bowl from his sleeping father's grasp. Ten hours later, in the dark of morning, while his wife holds his hand and strokes his hair, Doc dies. The championship trophy stands on the sideboard. Doc campaigned for a final victory—and won it!

A Navy color guard came to Doc's front yard and stood under the great camphor tree—rigid, stone-jawed. They read their eulogies, fired their salute, and gave Ba the American flag.

I'm glad they did, but for me I'll always remember what Doc said one time we were out training his string of Kapalaea setters. "Bill," he said, "so many fine things have happened to me. So many titles. So many uniforms. But you know, those whistles that hang on my neck—those two dog training whistles—are a badge of honor to me. I'd rather have those whistles hanging there and *feel* I have a right to wear them than to display any other honors I ever received. Those two dog whistles are, quite frankly, bigger than the two admiral stars I once wore."

I stand from the typewriter and turn to stare at the two admiral stars Ba has sent me. I've stuck them on a ribbon I won at a field trial somewhere. I touch them. I turn. Is this what 1985 is to be? Another year in which my very life—the loves of my life—is further reduced. A world in which everything I value continues to slip away.

I'm standing there feeling lost and left behind when Dee enters the room, carrying the mail, cheering the day. For Dee is like a springer's tail: always happy. I take the mail in grumble and sit to read one letter after another. There's a dog eating birds in Georgia. A retriever in Minnesota won't come when called. A cocker in Utah has a rare skin rash. Then I open a letter postmarked Elizabethtown, Kentucky. The letter is written on lined paper with a lead pencil. The writer says he is a seventeen-year-old boy named Nathan Barnes. Nathan has a pretty good hand. And he draws two very good bobwhite quail at the bottom of the page. Nathan tells me, "I'm new at quail hunting and training bird dogs, but with your help I know I can have a good hunting dog.

"I live in a great quail country, with lots of corn and soybean crops all around my house, so I'll have good places to hunt and train my Brittany spaniel (Rusty). This is my first bird dog. He was given to me by a man who owned him since he was a pup. He was about 4 months old when I got him.

"When I received the pup he'd been hit by a car and was skinny. My brother-in-law brought him to me because he knew I was wanting a Brittany. He had checked Rusty and saw he didn't have any broken bones or any serious injury. He was just very weak and his upper legs were bruised up. After a couple of weeks and lots of love and care, Rusty started getting up and moving around, but he couldn't use his back legs very well. Now I've had him two months and he's doing great. We go romping in the fields behind my house and he loves chasing rabbits and jumping quail and woodcock or any other kind of bird."

I straighten in my typing chair, jump back to the top of the page and read it all again. This is the stuff America's made of: a down-home kid and a hard-luck dog.

Nathan goes on to tell me that if I'll answer a few questions he can correct some of Rusty's problems. Then he lists the problems and closes his letter by writing, "Love ya, Nathan."

I take paper from the pile beside me and slide it fresh and new and blank into the typewriter. The letters start running, the words pile up, the lines cascade down. I'm writing to Nathan. And I'm feeling good. Things are looking up. Why hell, things are going to be all right. I say backwards in smile, I say to Doc's stars on the wall behind me, "Ol' pardner, we remember another seventeen-year-old kid, don't we? Or the kid said he was seventeen, right?" I'm talking to Doc with my mind, and my hands are just sizzling the words out to Nathan in Elizabeth-town, Kentucky.

And all the juices are boiling, and all the life forces are knocking things out of their way, and well, heck . . . Happy 1986 to all of you, it's going to be a swell year. Matter of fact, I know for certain it's going to be the best year you and I ever had.

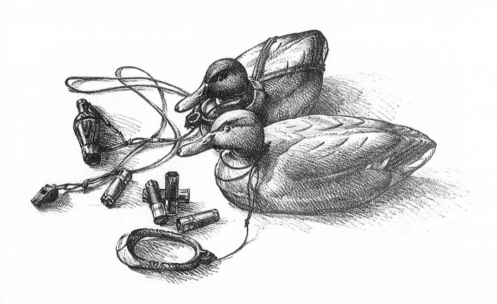

19

The Hunting Guide

When you release a story to the world, it takes on a life of its own—and it's hard to predict what that will be. But the public will let you know. The letters start coming, the phone starts ringing. Or nothing happens at all.

When this story hit the doorsteps and magazine racks, a host of hunters said they had to hunt with this man. The crack of light we put on this Texas quail guide had become a mega-lumen of glare.

Bud Daniel is one part gun dog trainer and one part grassroots philosopher. Not only is his job to train up gun dogs you can shoot over, but he entertains you while you're doing it.

This 6-foot, 2-inch, 226-pound combination Arkansas native and Texas migrant (let me explain that: he trains in Arkansas during the hot summer months and hunts bobwhite in South Texas during bird season) says of himself, "I'm like a mule. I have no pride of ancestry and no hope for posterity." You got to be country folk to recall mules can't throw beget.

And that's the way Daniel carries on, saying such things as, "Never hire a man who wears a straw hat or smokes a pipe; he's forever chasing that damned hat or packing that damned pipe." His wisdom is deep and rustic—always with a touch of humor—and he makes a master hunting host. Here how this works.

He can be an independent contractor, booking his own hunts, catch as catch can. Or he can contract with a business that wants to entertain customers, award employees, and develop new clients. Such firms rent the lease, buy the truck, furnish the noon meal, and do whatever else pleases them. Bud shows up at the lease gate at sunrise and waits for the sports. When they arrive, he takes them hunting over at least twelve bird dogs he'll carry at all times so there'll always be a fresh brace down.

"My job is to accommodate the customer," says Bud, "and I put down sure'nuf trained bird dogs, conditioned, field and bird wise, with plenty of bottom in them to get the job done. You know in South Texas if the scenting conditions are poor, then that means the birds have flown ahead. We don't have a wind, we don't have a breeze—we've got a southeastern drift, and we develop dogs that can work on that paucity of help.

"But we've got the birds. Why, I've moved as many as thirty-seven coveys of bobwhite in one afternoon. The other day, we stopped by a windmill for lunch. And while they were putting the trash in tote sacks I let two dogs loose. Before we left that windmill we got into eight coveys. And when I say we ran into thirty-seven coveys you've got to realize we were delayed mightily by the gunners getting off and back on the hunting truck."

Daniel, who played pulling guard at Arkansas in a single-wing formation, and surprisingly has a degree in forestry (I look around for a tree), starts talking about today's guy and his gun dog. He says, "Dogs are better than they've ever been; it's people who aren't what they used to be. Most dogs have been bred now to the point of where they have all of the best in inherent qualities. But most people who own these high-bred dogs usually have a job somewhere and can only train or bird hunt on a weekend. Now these dogs are taken care of feedwise, and medically, and they're in excellent shape as far as everything but being conditioned. The guy lets the dog loose on a weekend and by Sunday night he's not even started to get the edge off.

"Used to be, when the dogs stayed up under the house, you walked out with your shotgun and let the bolt fly, the dogs come out from under there ready to go. It was over the fence at a real leisurely gait; they had finding birds on their minds instead of seeing what was on the other side of that ridge because they had already seen what was on the other side of that ridge.

"And we say those oldtime dogs were better bird dogs. They weren't. We're just not the people that we used to be because our lives are geared different. Nobody has the chance to live on the land and get out to the fields each day. And that's what a gun dog needs.

"Shucks, there ain't nothing to breaking a bird dog. South Texas is such a wonderful place because you can sit there on that hunting truck, and that dog can go through covey after covey. He'll make all his mistakes, and keep making them over and over, and you know just as soon as he's cleared that one there's another one over there just a few steps. And that's not just with one dog, that may be with four or five down. That running lets them get all those mistakes out of their system.

"It's not like Arkansas, where I come from, where we've gone from a small subsistence-farming-patch economy to one that's oriented toward large ownership, primarily timber. We still have a lot of birds in the woods—more than you'd probably think and a lot more than you'll probably see. But to try and break a pup up there where you can't see him at all times and you only hear a whir and see a blur? You scream, 'Where did he go?' 'Did the puppy flush him?' 'I don't know.' 'Well, catch him and whip him anyway.'

"And it may be until tomorrow afternoon before you see another covey of birds. We'll take two years to break a young dog up there, but we can do that in less than sixty days down here with a good dog that's mature enough to be ready to break. You can do more with him down here in two years time than anywhere else, except Kansas.

"But even there, ownership patterns restrict what you are able to do and what you want to do. But down here it is so easy. You're sitting on that truck most of the time. And you see forever and ever. Dogs learn to handle because they need a drink of water as much as anything else. And they learn to come to the truck. You can do your culling on a lot different basis down here. In South Texas, the first thing you look for in a dog that's ready to break is bottom. That is—if he's got the go, he can't help but intercept birds. In Arkansas and Kansas, a dog has to learn where birds live. He's got to learn to go to the edges. He can run to the middle of some of those places up there in that rolling prairie and turn around and look at you as if to say, 'What am I doing here?'

"Now, a dog broke in Arkansas and brought to Texas does a good job because the birds are everywhere and he doesn't have to find them. There are edges down here, but they are not as clearly defined. But at the same time, a dog broke in Texas and taken to Arkansas still has to learn. Because he's got to learn to go to the edges, he's got to learn all about heavy cover. He'll go over and he'll start jumping and looking at you like he's saying, 'How much farther do we have to go before we start to hunt?'

"And that is one of the differences. But back to what I wanted to emphasize. You don't have to do a lot of yelling and hacking down here to train a dog. That dog knows where you are, and you know where he is, and you keep pushing. The one that does not turn into a bird dog is the exception. And you don't have to beat him into it, you're not going to do any good beating him down here. They finally figure out if they don't move on point the birds won't move in a lot of cases. But if they do move, the birds are going to move. And when you start shooting birds in front of them and they get their mouth on a bird while fetching, you've got it made."

We're yard training dogs today, check-cording them into a hobbled pigeon's scent cone. This is not the way Bud works. He's all for getting dogs into natural birds. But he's consented to help me test something, and we're also having a good photo session. Finally Bud says, "You know it's birds that make a bird dog. Like me. I was always meant to be a banker, but nobody got me into money. How could I be a banker with no money? Same with these dogs. How can they be a bird dog with no birds?

"And you can't worry about things," he says. "Years ago I was in the pulpwood business and my whole living depended on ground conditions. If it rained, we were out of business; we couldn't get out of the woods. I spent half of my time concerned about the wood job because it was wet weather, or winter, or something like that. I thought *the perfect way to solve this is to plant me a big corn crop.* That way, if it's wet, then I'll be glad for the corn, and if it's dry, I'll be glad for the wood job. But the outcome was I ruined what half-time I had. When it was wet, I worried about the wood job, and when it was dry, I worried about the damned corn. So do your best with your dog and don't worry about it. But I do advise you to get him into tons of wild birds."

Bud brings a dog into the bird's scent cone and says over to me, "Don't pay too much attention to so-called experts. The other day a man went to the doctor and told him his left leg hurt. The doctor laughed and said, 'Why that's just old age.' The patient replied, 'Like hell it is. My other leg's the same age and it don't hurt.'"

Then Bud walks up to me and says, "I like dogs. They respond to the care that I give them, they are faithful. I like them because every time I go to get them they do what they are supposed to do. Not a one of them ever said, 'I don't want to go.' And when I get through with them and put them away, not a one of them says, 'Where you going when you leave here?' And when I get back, there isn't a one of them that asks, 'Where you been?'"

"I want to ask you something," I say. "There's a theory that bird dogs smell quail breath. Got any ideas on that?"

"Yeah. I don't believe it. What I do believe is bird dogs smell bob-white droppings. I guarantee you get a covey rise or a couple of birds get up out there that a dog's got pointed and you watch them . . . they'll go fifty, sixty yards and they'll dump in the air. You've seen 'em. Now the dog hasn't seen that, okay? But when he crosses that track where those droppings fell he'll shut down just a second, then pick up and go on.

"If birds are in one place and have been there for any period—3 or 4 minutes—they're easily detected by the dog. But if a bird just went in, and there's enough cover to hold him—we used to call him 'air-washed'—even though we saw the bird go in, when the dog goes in he can't smell him for anything. And finally we kick the bird up and the dog hasn't smelled him and we say the dog is no good . . . he has no nose. I'll say there wasn't something there for him to smell. I say there were no droppings for him to cue in on."

The day is done and I'm leaving Bud when he yells at me, "We ought to farm like in Biblical times. The vow required you leave so much for the gleaners; the edges had to be left, and the poor were allowed to come into the fields after the wealthy had gathered the crops they were allowed to gather. That's what I think it ought to go back to instead of farming fence-row to fence-row with quail carrying their lunch across a lot of those fields."

I wave at him, climb in my car, and pull out. A day with Bud Daniel is a treat. No wonder he's become bobwhite's master host.

20

ANOTHER BEND IN THE RIVER

In closing this book, we find a Lab pup and me walking a frozen and meandering river for ducks. Every hunter has had a day like this. And I pray to God those who follow will have the same day, too.

God intended man live like this—as he has for 12,000 recorded years.

Those deluded and mentally truncated misfits—in essence, those naturalist eunuchs—who want to outlaw guns and hunting and using dogs to work have never known truth and beauty and have never felt that feeling each of us know when we've fitted correctly into the palm of God, into His scheme of life, into His plan for man, land, and animal.

The Prairie mind is inflexibly simple and correct. It cannot acknowledge the Arkansas River being pronounced any other way. Up at the river's headwaters, high in the Rockies, people may mistakingly call it the Arkansa(w). And down in the state of Arkansa(w), where the river empties into the Mississippi, those people may lose their (s) and say it the same way. But when that river enters Kansa(s), we hold to that (s) ending with the grip of a badger. If we didn't, then our state would be Kansa(w), and that would be unimaginable.

The farm ponds in Kansas are frozen now, and the waterfowl on the open refuges seldom leave their government handouts to forage the storm-shattered and snow-ladened fields. So the fifteen-month-old black Lab pup I call Happy walks the banks of the Arkansas River with me, up by Great Bend, Kansas. For the river makes a great bend here, and like ant trails that bend this way or that, you can never reason its going. And though the river is frozen in sections, still there are open spots where a chance duck may idle and feed.

Happy rambles with that rolling of baby fat about his shoulders, the snow and ice on his coat glistening in the bright but heatless sun. Happy doesn't know why we're out here—why we're not hidden in the hay bales by the farm pond or sneaking corners of this shallow river in the old johnboat with the bottom slicked by the scum of stinkbait and the rusted metal fish stringer still snapped to the oar lock.

At those spots where the bank is nearly level with the river, Happy runs down to wade in the water midst floating ice to drink. Where the bank is high and undercut, he stands and looks quizzically at the brown swirls, his mind still vacant about what he sees.

The earth is frozen, and where the wind's blown it clean of snow I walk without drag, the Christmas parka in winter-camo pattern prompting me to see myself as a snow leopard. Thought of the big cat brings an imagined spring to my step, puts me up on my toes.

The heft of the Remington automatic swings easily in my right hand. It'll mount in a second, swing as fast. It'll bark and bite and a red-legged mallard (the red legs are always last to come down from Canada) will lie flat on his back in the water, and Happy will have to hope that's where the bank meets the river. Happy's unsure about leaping from a high bank.

But the pup's signed on as a gun dog, and he'll have to meet life as the hunter finds it: The hours of nothing, the seconds of plenty—the clear shot, the shot deflected through gnarled cottonwood limbs, the birds flying close to the cut bank, not to clear for fifty yards before they lift. And who's got a gun that can shoot fifty yards? Oh, I may have done it once or twice.

I labor under a four-strand barbed wire fence (no longer a lithe snow leopard), to leave behind the frozen winter wheatfield. There'll be cattle here, but Happy won't tend to them. He's learned that since puppyhood while we were out in the fields Happy Timing. There's nothing harder to walk in than a pasture where cattle have sunk in during heavy rains; the frozen escarpments always catch a toe of your boot and plunge you forward. And the wire fence now runs along the river bank, so Happy will have to duck under to make any retrieve. But he's learned that Happy Timing, too.

Matter of fact, Happy knows it all: all the cover and terrain and hazards and distractions. That's what we learned all summer walking in the idle fields. All Happy doesn't know is the red-legged mallard floating upside down in the water.

I kneel and call the pup to side, telling him in serious voice to stay low, not to kick out sideways, not to go on a lark. For the bend in the river lies just ahead—there'll be a stretch of open water there. The ducks will feed against the bank out of the wind, and any sentinel they post will be able to see everywhere except over the cut bank. So dog and man must always slink around bends in rivers. They must disappear. Yet, all humped over, how can a man move fast? For when the ducks do sense your presence they'll scat, since they've got this all figured out. They know the gun. They've met guns all the way from Canada to Kansas. They are experts on guns. They know how long it takes to shoulder them, how far they shoot, how wide their pattern.

All I've done is walk hunched over and I'm winded. Still, Happy and I move quickly forward, his puppy mind sensing this is different, this is serious. His puppy eyes are no longer vacant; they are intense about he does not know what. And suddenly they're on us: that's right, not us on them but them on us. A flight of seven mallards has cut across my left shoulder; they were making their way for the open water and must have been daydreaming, for they tried to set down right beside us. And now the gun won't raise nor sweep in a second, and when it's finally up it won't shoot. I forget the safety. And Happy's running after the ducks. The flying-away ducks.

And I can't believe it. But I must. Always it's this way. For that's hunting. To have everything planned, and then it's you who gets blown out of the water. It is myself I see float belly up in my snow leopard coat down the murky river.

But I can't think of that! Happy's turned from the flying ducks and now runs straight toward a herd of cattle. The ducks never saw me, I never saw the Herefords. I'm on the whistle, telling Happy to come back when right from below me, right from the cut bank I was to have stalked, spring up three mallards in grating voice and a fountain of water. They hang in the air before me like tethered balloons. They can't gain loft, their wings miss the wind, and I am paralyzed. The whole world laughs at me. The ducks, the cattle, and Happy all laugh, for that's how Happy got his name.

And now the cattle come charging in that straight-legged way they have. Only I'm not laughing. I don't take to unraveling all that well, to see precision dragged out by dry bearings, to see the whole engine of life explode. So I run straight at the cattle, giving a call the Kiowa must have yelled at buffalo. And it looks like we're going to collide when suddenly the cattle feel they're in the presence of a bona fide idiot and they swing off, churning the frozen ground to lift in fist-sized clods. Now Happy can chase them. And I blow the whistle.

I sit on the dried, chunked mud and wait for Happy to run out his string. Finally he comes, covered with the foam of his lust, his tongue hanging limp. I can't scold him. I introduced him to cattle when Happy Timing, but I never put him behind a stampede. He goes past me to the river and walks midst the ice floes to drink. But he looks back with too much white in his eyes. He is concerned about me. I may scold him. So I must shake it off for both of us. I toss a dried cow chip out behind him, and he leaps and pumps to make the retrieve.

But the cow chip goes with the water's current, and suddenly Happy goes faster than he can swim. He tries to turn toward the bank, but he enters swirls, and I can imagine all those forces as they press against him. Yet, he snatches the cow chip and leaps from the water to his waist, then twists and turns toward the bank, crabbing now to come in straight. I never taught him that. Survival put that in him. I take the slickened cow chip from his mouth and drop it to the ground, covering it with my boot, telling him, "No." But I must push his head back with my other boot. Finally he looks into my eyes for a long time, then turns and ambles to go shake water, a rainbow of light arching about his shoulders.

I should let him rest a minute, so I pat my pockets to find the candy bar. I chew on it as I look off to the horizon, off to the grain elevators that accent the flat prairie floor from Texas to Canada. They look like great silver trophies erected to the farmer and his kin. But that was before man and nature devastated the farmer. Now the silos stand as tombstones.

There were two American statesmen who knew about these grain elevators, though they never saw one. Throughout their political lives they maintained a running debate both bitter and crucial.

Alexander Hamilton said the future of America was the city artisan, the shopkeeper, their urban interests would both foster and protect a strong national government. Thomas Jefferson pleaded, "No, the future of this land lies in the hands of the family farmer and home rule. That is the basis of democracy. Lose them and you lose it all."

I'm thinking about naming my next dog Jefferson when I give Happy the last bite of candy and cast out with an empty hand, telling him to "Hie on." He leaps high to tap my chest with his front paws and twists to come down going away from me. Running now.

Again the gun rests easy in my hand. Again my steps grow certain. But still, I glance back now and then. I've been ambushed once. And I see the cattle move up slowly on a knoll to watch after us. They were ambushed, too.

Happy runs happy after he knows not what. And I pick up my pace knowing game cannot be far away. For there's always another bend in the river.